Taste
of Totterdown

A Community Cookbook
Written by the People of Totterdown

TOTTERDOWN *PRESS*

Published by Totterdown Press in 2008

Totterdown Press is an imprint of Tangent Books
Unit 5.16, Paintworks
Arnos Vale
Bristol BS4 3EH

0117 972 0645
www.tangentbooks.co.uk

Copyright Tangent Books 2008

Compiled by: **Mia Harris, Richard Jones**
Photography: **Natalie Corfield**
Consultant Editor: **Francine Russell**
Cover Cake Decoration: **Tina Shearer**
Photography Assistant: **Shona Graham**
Design: **Joe Burt**
Production: **Anne Scott**
Publisher: **Richard Jones**
Thanks to: **Percy J Down at Bristol Fruit Market, Carolyn Jones**
Special thanks to: **Kate Pollard**

Natalie Corfield has asserted her right under the Copyright, Designs and Patents Act of 1988 to be identified as the photographer of this work. Pictures are available to download free of charge at www.tasteoftotterdown.co.uk

Taste of Totterdown community cookbook was published as part of the 'Totterdown in Print' project with the aid of an Awards For All lottery grant awarded to Totterdown Residents Environmental & Social Action, community interest company.

Special thanks are due to Kate Pollard for her dedication and enthusiasm in writing the original grant proposal; to all who played a part in bringing it to fruition; and, of course, to everyone in Totterdown's wonderfully diverse, and occasionally eccentric, community who contributed recipes.

LOTTERY FUNDED

Contents

Welcome to Taste of Totterdown

Creating this book has been a wonderful and exciting collaboration involving many parts of the community of Totterdown. You have invited us into your homes and businesses and been so generous with your time, allowing us to photograph you with your selected dishes. Totterdown is a vibrant and diverse community and this is reflected in the pages ahead.

From the outset, recipes with poignant personal stories, anecdotes or with historical or religious significance have flooded in and made the experience of putting together a community cookery book hugely enjoyable.

One thing that is apparent for many who have contributed to this book is that the joy in cooking is not only in creating the dish but also in the experience of sharing it.

As you turn the pages, you'll find examples of delicious recipes that have been created for this book, or that have been handed down through generations of families – recipes that have accompanied people who have settled here and recipes that are cooked and served in local eateries. Whatever their origin, we can be assured that food is far more than just fuel for the body and the process of cooking is not just a means to an end.

Food in all of its forms is our common ground. It may sound like a cliché but all of us must eat, and if we can be social in the process then all the better.

Food has a massive impact on our lives whether we realise it or not.

What sits on the plate is as much a slave to fickle fashion as what hangs in our wardrobe. It seems we are told on a daily basis to buy organic, buy local, buy slow, eat fast, eliminate something, buy the latest superfood, or buy into a fad diet that will have incredible health-changing benefits. It is all so confusing and perhaps there's too much information?

What we really seem to be moving towards is getting back to the basics that were the every day norm for generations before us. Food education, where food comes from, growing food and learning about a balanced diet has now become an integral part of a school day, resulting in increasing young people's skills and knowledge as early as four or five years old. Education in a different format is also conveyed via the power of the media. Massive audiences watch celebrity chefs make food and make food preparation 'sexy' and theatrical. This has resulted in the appeal of food and cookery being widely acknowledged and accepted by people young and old who would not have been the usual foodie suspects a few years ago.

In a fast-paced world, preparing and cooking food can sometimes seem like too much hard work. But the preparation of food is an art form that involves all five of our senses: the texture of food, the colour, the smells, the sounds (like the first time you break the caramel layer of a crème brulée), not to mention the taste. Food nostalgia and memories stay with us throughout life. Childhood flavours and smells leave their mark and the foods of our youth often become a source of solace later in life. When we are down in the dumps, food can be a comfort and when we have reason to celebrate, food is often at the centre of an event.

Eating communally is thankfully the one thing that we haven't been able to master remotely and electronically. It means we can enjoy shared conversation, rituals and foods that strengthen our common bonds as friends, families and as communities.

Because of the centrality of food in our lives, many cultures and religions have feast days and fast days, and may list acceptable and prohibited foods. Special occasions, from funerals to weddings, are all life-changing events accompanied by symbolic offerings of food. If you think of any really special event you have attended or look back at photos of a special occasion, food will generally be the focal point. Ritual, foods and meals mean we are marking an occasion and making it a special event.

Cooking has many meanings to me, but ultimately it is about food made with love that brings people together and creates memories. Food is a way of enabling the past to be alive in the present. We hope you will enjoy replicating and sampling the delicious, diverse and

interesting recipes in this book. In doing so, you are keeping alive the stories and history that comes with them.

Francine Russell, Arnos Street, 2008

Francine Russell

Francine Russell is All About Food – a consultant and trainer with more than 20 years' experience of the food sector. She designs courses for the public and voluntary sector with a strong emphasis on healthier approaches to cooking, eating and living. Her work includes delivering programmes for a cross-section of communities and

frequently in partnership with Bristol Primary Care Trust, Bristol City Council and The Healthy Schools Team. Francine's formal training includes a degree in Hotel Management, cooking diploma from The Cordon Bleu School, Advanced Diploma in Nutrition, Bournemouth University and a Diploma in Teaching. Until 2007 Francine had her own café in Bristol.

In addition, she now provides delicious and healthy food from her catering company and is Slow Food recommended. Francine can be found at the Bristol Slow Food monthly market in Corn Street.

Further information at www.allaboutfood.uk.com

STARTERS SNACKS & BREADS

Pumpkin and Coconut Soup with Harissa

Origin
North African.

Recipe supplied by
Sarah Jasna Heubach who runs Organique, Wells Road Totterdown.

Ingredients
1 tbsp olive oil
1 onion, finely chopped
1 kg pumpkin or butternut squash, peeled and cubed
600 ml hot vegetable stock
400 ml coconut milk
1 tbsp harissa paste
Coriander, finely chopped

For me, food plays a key role in creating culture, landscape and health. This inspired me to create Organique – a local food store for the communities of Totterdown and Knowle. I saw it as an opportunity to participate in placing the interests of the local community, the environment and our health as directors of our food systems, as opposed to a system that best serves the interests of a centralised industry.

Method
1. Heat the oil in a large pan over medium heat.
2. Cook the onion until brown and slightly crispy.
3. Add the harissa paste, stirring.
4. Then add stock and the pumpkin.
5. Bring to boil and simmer till pumpkin is tender (approx 15 mins).
6. Blend the soup.
7. Return to the pan and add the coconut milk.
8. Season to taste and gently heat through.
9. Garnish with coriander and serve.

Smoked Paprika and Kidney Bean Soup

Origin
Bristolian.

Recipe supplied by
Naomi Berry of Oxford Street who has lived in Totterdown since 2000.

Ingredients
2 tsp olive oil
2 medium onions, chopped
2 fat cloves of garlic
1 tbsp smoked sweet paprika (if you use hot version reduce amount of cayenne)
2 tsp ground cumin
2 tsp cayenne pepper
2 tsp ground coriander
1 can drained red kidney beans
1 can tomatoes
2 tbsp tomato puree
1 litre of stock
Pot of sour cream or crème fraiche
Flat leaf parsley
Herbert's overnight baguette
Garlic butter

Serves four.
Cooking time: 30 mins.
Blender needed.

Fast food and a store cupboard classic. This supa soup will be recalled with affection from the Front Room Art Trail of 2006.

Method
1. Sauté chopped onions slowly in oil, until they are soft and translucent but not brown.
2. Reduce heat and stir in chopped garlic then all the spices.
3. Stir spices until they start to release smells after 30 seconds or so.
4. Slosh in beans, tomatoes, puree and stock.
5. Bring to the boil then reduce heat and simmer for 30 mins.
6. Taste and season then blitz with blender stick until you have chunky smooth supa soup.
7. Garnish with dollop of sour cream and chopped flat-leaf parsley.

TOP TIP
Serve with toasted Herbert's overnight baguette and garlic butter. Mmmm.

Prawns on Potato Rosti

Origin
Bristolian.

Recipe supplied by
Geordie Johnnie of
Cemetery Road,
Totterdown.

Ingredients
1 lb raw prawns – tiger
are best but large pink
will do
2 green avocados
(Haas avocados go a
wee bit runny)
8 medium-sized fleshy
potatoes
½ onion
6 cloves garlic
2 tbsp butter
2 tbsp crème fraiche
1 lime
2 small birds eye chillies
2 tbsp olive oil

Serves four.

An original experiment which turned out rather well!

Method

1. Boil the hell out of the potatoes which should be sliced into roughly 1 inch pieces – about 25 minutes is best.
2. Put the olive oil in a frying pan. Heat until nearly smoking and put in the roughly chopped onion and 3 finely chopped garlic cloves. Sauté until soft – don't burn the garlic because it'll go sour.
3. When the potatoes are soft, mash them with the soft onions and fried garlic. Leave to one side to cool. Don't throw your oil out as it'll have a lovely oniony/garlicky edge to it now.
4. Skin and stone the avocados. Crush the remaining garlic. Chuck it all in a big dish and mash with a fork – (a good one! Some tend to bend like you're Uri Geller when you use them!) Add a splash of olive oil if they're being stubborn.
5. Take a handful of cold mash potato/onion/garlic mix and shape like a snowball into 4 x 4 inch diameter 'patties'. Fry these in a new frying pan (you'll need the old one for your prawns) until they are gold and crispy on the outside.
6. Finely chop the chillies and soften on a low heat in the oniony/garlicky oil. Blast up the heat and fry off the prawns. As soon as they lose their transparency they're done. Don't overcook them. Just as they're finishing cut the lime in half and squeeze over the juice of one half of lime.
7. Put the potato patty on a plate. Smooth over a good dollop of avocado mix. Spoon a quarter of the prawns over the top making sure you drizzle a generous quantity of the limey oil over each portion. Top with a spoonful of crème fraiche. The rest of the lime can be squeezed over the dish. Garnish with some fresh herbs (coriander is good).
8. Enjoy with a very cold, very dry white wine – oooh baby!

Beany Pinwheels

Origin
Bristol.

Recipe supplied by
Hillcrest Primary School,
School Road, Totterdown.

Ingredients
190 g white bread mix
63 g brown bread mix
100 g baked beans
176 ml (approx) water
320 g grated cheese for topping
100 g tomato coulis (pasta sauce)

Makes 10 portions.

The school was first opened in the 1870s and in 1999 Knowle Infants and Knowle Primary were amalgamated to create Hillcrest as it is now. The school is twinned with Kigumba Primary School in Uganda – both schools have allotments where they are learning to grown their own food.

Method
1. Make up bread as per pack instructions. At the end of the process mix in drained baked beans and mix until beans are evenly dispersed and have broken down.
2. Portion into 10 blocks and roll out into oblong shapes, spread with tomato coulis and sprinkle with the grated cheese.
3. Roll up and cut into even-sized pieces. Place cut side down on a lightly greased baking tray and allow to prove until double in size.
4. Bake in oven at 190 –200°C (gas mark 5-6) for 10-15 mins.

PICTURE: *Children collect fresh vegetables from the allotment at Hillcrest School.*

ckpea Snack (Chaat)

Origin
India.

Recipe supplied by
Vishnu who has lived in Totterdown all his life among a large Asian Christian family dotted around the area. He has been cooking since the mid 90s.

Ingredients
1 tsp chilli powder
400 g/14 oz can chickpeas, drained
2 medium potatoes
½ bunch of coriander, finely chopped
1 medium cucumber
1 tsp salt
1 tsp sugar
1 onion, chopped
2 tbsp tamarind paste
2 tbsp cumin
Chopped tomatoes and chillies to garnish

This dish is popular all over India. I find the canned sort of chickpeas very easy to use without sacrificing too much flavour.

Method
1. Place the drained chickpeas in a bowl.
2. Dice the potatoes and boil until cooked.
3. Mix together the tamarind paste and some water in a small mixing bowl to make a paste.
4. Add the chilli powder, sugar and the salt to the tamarind paste and mix together.
5. Pour the mixture over the chickpeas.
6. Add the onion, the cumin and the diced potatoes.
7. Stir to mix and transfer to serving bowl and garnish with chopped tomatoes and chillies.

Quick Hummus

Origin
Greek.

Recipe supplied by
Natalie Corfield from Margate Street who has lived in the Totterdown area since 2003.

Ingredients
200 g/7 oz canned chickpeas
2 tbsp lemon juice or more
2 garlic cloves, crushed
1 tsp ground cumin
Salt
100 ml/3.5 fl oz tahini (sesame seed paste)
4 tbsp water
2 tbsp extra virgin olive oil
1 tsp paprika
4 rounds of pitta bread

Method
1. Drain the chickpeas and rinse. Reserve a few whole chickpeas for serving.
2. Combine the chickpeas, lemon juice, garlic, cumin, salt, tahini and water in a food processor and whizz to a creamy purée.
3. Add more lemon juice, garlic, cumin or salt to taste. Turn out onto a dinner plate, and make smooth with the back of a spoon. Drizzle with extra virgin olive oil and scatter with the reserved chickpeas.
4. Sprinkle with paprika and serve with toasted pitta bread.

Chilli Popcorn

Origin
Bristol.

Recipe supplied by
Sarah Jasna Heubach from Organique, Wells Road, Totterdown.

Ingredients
230 g of popcorn
Oil for popping the corn
85 g unsalted butter
1 tiny clove of garlic
1 tsp zest from an unwaxed lemon
¼ tsp dried chilli flakes
Pinch of chilli powder
1 tsp black cracked pepper
1 tsp sea salt

This is a quick and easy snack with a kick. Go as hot as you dare with the chilli.

Method
1. Pop the corn in very hot oil. Set aside.
2. Melt the butter in a pan over a medium heat, adding the garlic and lemon zest, chilli flakes and chilli powder and black pepper.
3. Pour all the popcorn into a large serving bowl and pour over flavoured butter, season with salt and mix well.

Fried Cheese ("Smažený sýr" or "Smažák")

Origin
Czech Republic.

Recipe supplied by
Jan Turnovský from the Czech Republic who works at Cartridge World, Wells Road, Totterdown.

Ingredients
2-3 slices of Edam cheese, approx 1 cm thick bread crumbs
Plain flour
1-2 eggs
Salt
Sunflower oil
Potatoes
Carraway seeds (optional)
Mayonnaise

This very popular low-cost meal is available in the majority of Czech pubs and inns.

Method
1. Cut the Edam into slices and get ready three bowls: the first one with plain flour, the second one with 1-2 eggs mixed with a fork, the third one with breadcrumbs.
2. Boil halved potatoes with optional addition of some carraway seeds until potatoes are soft.
3. Cover the whole surface of the cheese slice with flour. Do not forget to cover its sides, then place it into the bowl with eggs, cover completely, put the slice into the breadcrumbs using the fork and cover the slice with breadcrumbs.
4. Fry the cheese in hot oil until soft.
5. Serve with potatoes and mayonnaise.

TOP TIP
There is no better way of serving this than with a pint of cold Czech lager.

Batika Vada Potato Snack

Origin
India.

Recipe supplied by
Kirti Patel, Cambridge Street,
Totterdown.

Ingredients
For the filling
1 lb potatoes, boiled and mashed
1 onion, finely chopped
Chilli, ginger and garlic paste to taste
Bunch fresh coriander, chopped
Salt to taste
Sugar to taste
1 tsp mustard seeds and sesame seeds
Lemon juice, according to preference
2 tbsp oil

For the batter
2 cups gram flour
1 tsp fruit salt
Pinch of salt to taste
Water
Vegetable oil for frying

This is a lovely spicy potato snack. The spices for this are available from Patco.

Method
1. Heat 2 tbsp of oil in a pan. Add the mustard and sesame seeds.
2. When seeds start to pop, add the onions and allow to cook till tender. Add this to the mashed potato.
3. Now add chilli, ginger and garlic paste and the rest of the ingredients. Mix well and divide the mixture into small round balls.
4. To form batter, mix the gram flour, fruit salt, normal salt and water until it's just like a pancake batter.
5. Heat some oil in a pan for frying. Add 2 tbsp of hot oil into the batter and mix well. Now take each ball individually, dip it into the batter and drop into the hot oil and deep fry on low heat until golden brown. Do this with all the mixture.
6. Serve hot with tomato ketchup.

SELECT YOUR OWN

PEPPERS House
GRADE I
£2·08 #
6·58p

Chillies.
£1·20
a pocket.
CLASS I
THAILAND.

Garlic & Ginger
£3·85 kg
China - class I

ali wa Nazi (Coconut Rice)

Origin
Kenya.

Recipe supplied by
Maggie Telfer, who is Director of Bristol Drugs Project. She lived in Richmond Street in the mid 80s for two years and has lived in Balmain Street since 1999.

Ingredients
¼ kg uncooked rice
Grated white meat of 1 large or 2 small coconuts
Water and salt

In 1996, I first visited Kenya to help set up the Omari Project – a rehabilitation centre for problem drug users just outside Malindi on the East Kenyan Coast. I spent at least a month every year in Kenya for the next ten years. There are a lot of fish dishes on the Kenyan coast, but I'm a vegetarian so I've chosen my favourite veggie recipe from the Malindi area. This coconut rice is prepared by women who sit on a special stool with a blade sticking out of the front on which they grate the coconut.

Method
1. Cover the grated coconut with boiling water and squeeze out the first creamy thick milk. Put this aside.
2. Add more hot water and squeeze again to obtain a thinner milk. Wash the rice three times in cold water.
3. Put the thinner coconut milk in a saucepan with a little salt and let it nearly come to the boil. Add the washed rice and stir carefully. Keep stirring so as not to burn.
4. Add the creamy thick coconut milk and continue stirring. The heat must be moderate.
5. Cover the rice with greaseproof paper, put on the pan lid and a heavy weight to seal, and steam for about 25 mins on a very low heat until ready to serve.

Sherpa Fried Potatoes

Origin
Nepal.

Recipe supplied by
Lhamu, Viva Oliva, Oxford Street,
Totterdown.

Ingredients
Potatoes, peeled and cut into small chips
Garlic, chilli and salt made into a paste
Green dill leaves
Olive oil or mustard seed oil for frying

My father is a Sherpa and met Sir Edmund Hillary many times in the course of Hillary's work in Nepal. Much English cooking seems to embody boiling and loss of flavour! Most Nepalese food is fried in freshly ground spices in minimal amounts of oil and is very spicy and flavoursome, but not in a hot spicy kind of way. Sherpas live and work at high altitudes and have to be very fit.

Method

1. You can use olive oil but in Nepal freshly crushed mustard seed oil is used and this gives the potatoes their special flavour. You can make the mustard seed oil by putting the seed in a blender – UK commercial mustard oil doesn't taste right, so use olive oil if that's easier.

2. Heat the oil in a flat-bottomed pan until it is smoking. Add the potatoes and stir in the spice mix. Fry them from raw until they are cooked. Add more oil as required plus a dash of it at the end.

3. Then at the last moment, add the dill, stir it in and serve.

The Elvis Presley Sandwich

Origin
Chicago.

Recipe supplied by
Gerry King, Upper Street, Totterdown.

Ingredients
2 pieces of white bread
1 banana
Peanut butter
Butter
1 or 2 tsp jam (Jelly)
2 slices of bacon (narrow strips)

While staying with a 'Swing dancing' friend in Chicago some years ago I was privileged to consume the above sandwich. One evening; prior to going to the 'Smoke Daddy' (Tel: 773 772 MOJO) rhythm and bar-b-que lounge on Division Street, we cooked and ate 'The Elvis'. Video footage exists of the cooking and eating experience and from watching I can only say that a sense of contentment and happiness pervades the tout ensemble. This sandwich must be a shared experience or it could be construed as self-abuse within the 'Victorian' context.

Method
1. Fry off the bacon until crispy.
2. Spread peanut butter to desired depth on bread.
3. Slice the bananas enough to cover peanut butter and then stick them in the peanut butter.
4. Spread the jam over the bananas.
5. Place together and butter outside of bread.
6. Place in hot butter melted in a frying pan and cook on both sides until golden brown, but not too long – the peanut butter will be runny.
7. Place crispy bacon in sandwich and eat.

PICTURE: *Gerry King displays the ingredients for the Elvis Presley Sandwich helped by Alexi (left) and Mena.*

tcakes

This reminds me of buying ready-to-cook oatcakes in Derby market hall on Saturdays from a lovely old lady. It always makes me think of crisp, clear Autumn mornings in the country, with my brother and I getting up early on Sunday to go mushroom picking in the fields close to our house. Then we would all sit around to breakfast with all those lovely smells…

Origin
Derbyshire.

Recipe supplied by
Carolyn Jones, Green Street, Totterdown.

Ingredients
1 lb fine oatmeal
1 lb flour
2 pints warm water (approx)
1 oz sachet dried yeast
Pinch salt
Pinch sugar

Method

1. Mix together the oatmeal, flour and salt in a large bowl. Add a small amount of warm water to the yeast and sugar to form a creamy paste. Add a little more water so that you have a smooth liquid.
2. Pour the liquid yeast mixture into the dry ingredients and then slowly add the remaining water, mixing thoroughly until you have a thin batter.
3. Leave for 1 hour in a warm place for it to rise (bubbles will form on the surface).
4. While the batter is resting, prepare a Sunday feast to go on top of the oatcakes – mushrooms, eggs, tomatoes, cheese, fresh herbs, bacon if you must. Cook topping ingredients and keep warm.
5. To cook the oatcakes, lightly oil a large frying pan/griddle if you have one. Pour a ladleful of batter into the hot pan, swirl around to cover base and then cook for 4-5 minutes on each side. Should be the consistency of thick pancakes. Once crispy turn out onto a warmed plate and add your toppings.

Pickled onions

Origin
East London.

Recipe supplied by
Kim Woods, Upper Street,
Totterdown.

Ingredients
20 small onions or shallots
Spiced pickling vinegar

My brother Gary and I grew up in the East End of London and every year around September or October, mum would make delicious, crunchy pickled onions. Stored away in a dark cupboard until Christmas time, they made an excellent accompaniment to meat and cheeses. Now I live in Totterdown and continue the family tradition of home-made pickles.

Method
1. Peel the onions and soak in salted water for 1-2 hours*.
2. Pat dry and put into jars.
3. Pour spiced pickling vinegar on top until totally covered.

Many recipes recommend soaking the onions for up to 12 hours but this can make them soft. You only need to soak them long enough to get the juices out and I've found that between 1 and 2 hours is enough.

TOP TIP
Sometimes I add a handful of dried red chillis for an extra kick.

Soup Avgolemona and olive Bread

Origin
Greek.

Recipe supplied by
Natasha Gregory of
Greg's Cafe, Wells
Road, Totterdown.

A classic Greek recipe given to me from my mother-in-law with a refreshing tangy lemon flavour. The bread is an ideal Greek bread to accompany soup. You can use either black or green olives in the bread – black are definitely my favourite.

Soup
Ingredients
2.5 pints chicken stock
55 g short grain rice
2 eggs
6 tbsp freshly squeezed lemon juice
Sea salt and freshly ground pepper to season
Sliced lemon and chopped parsley to garnish

Serves: Four decent-sized bowls.

Method
1. Pour the stock into a large saucepan and bring to the boil. Add the rice and return to the boil and simmer for 15-20 mins or until rice is cooked.
2. Meanwhile, put the eggs and lemon juice into a bowl and whisk together.
3. When the rice is cooked, lower the heat and start stirring the stock and rice, ladle part of this mixture into the lemon juice and eggs. Once this has been mixed, pour the mixture back into the saucepan together with the chicken stock and rice. Continue to stir the mixture until the soup thickens. Tip: do not boil the mixture or it may curdle.
4. Season with salt and pepper.
5. Ladle the soup into the individual serving bowls and garnish each bowl with a slice of lemon and chopped parsley. This soup must be served hot.

PICTURE: *Natasha and the staff at Greg's Cafe on Wells Road.*

Olive Bread
Ingredients
900 g white flour
1 packet of yeast
3 tsp sesame seeds
1 tsp sea salt
½ tsp dried oregano
3 tbsp olive oil, plus extra for brushing
1 pint of warm water
225 g Greek olives, pitted, roughly chopped

Method
1. Put the flour, yeast and 2 tsp of sesasme seeds, the salt and oregano in a large bowl and mix. Add 3 tbsp of the olive oil and using a wooden spoon gradually add the water to form a firm dough.
2. Turn the dough onto a lightly floured work surface and knead for 10 mins until smooth.

Put the dough into a bowl and cover with a clean, damp tea towel and leave the dough to rise in a warm place for about 1 hour or until doubled in size.
3. Turn onto a lightly floured surface and knead lightly to knock out the air and then knead in the olives. Divide the dough into two pieces and shape into a smooth round loaf. Place on a lightly oiled baking tray, cover with a clean tea towel and leave in a warm place for about 30 mins until doubled in size.
4. Using a sharp knife, make slashes across the top of each loaf and lightly brush with olive oil and sprinkle with the remaining sesame seeds on top. Bake in a pre-heated oven on high for 10 mins and then reduce temperature to medium for a further 25 mins or until risen and brown and the bread sounds hollow when tapped on the bottom.

Challah - Jewish Sabbath Bread

Origin
Jewish.

Recipe supplied by
Francine Russell of All About Food.

Ingredients
2 tbsp dry yeast
500 ml lukewarm water
100 g sugar
4 eggs, beaten, plus 2 yolks or 1 whole egg for glazing
1 tbsp salt
125 ml vegetable oil
1.3 kg strong bread flour
Poppy/sesame seeds/ sunflower seeds (optional)

Makes four loaves.

PICTURE: *Francine Russell from Arnos Street making Challah with Maude Hardy and Mena Telfer from Balmain Street.*

Challah is a delicious, slightly sweet bread that resembles brioche. I was given this recipe by my friend Frances who had great fun making it with her 6-year-old daughter. I am sure it is one of Claudia Roden's – an author of several wonderful books on Jewish and middle-eastern cookery. Challah is not readily available in Bristol because there is not much of a Jewish community here. However, in north London on a Friday afternoon, you will find queues of people waiting impatiently to get their hands on some freshly baked challah ready for the Friday night family meal. It's delicious and keeps well for 2-3 days. As my mother would say "So try it already!"

Method

1. Dissolve the yeast in the water with 1 tsp of sugar. Beat well and leave 10 mins, until it froths.
2. In a very large bowl, lightly beat the eggs. Then add the salt, sugar, and oil and beat again. Add the frothy yeast mixture and beat well.
3. Now add the flour gradually – just enough to make a soft dough that holds together, mixing well, first with a large spoon, then working it in with your hands. Knead vigorously for about 15 minutes, until it is very smooth and elastic, adding flour if the dough is too sticky. Pour a little oil in the bowl and turn the dough, so that it is greased all over.
4. Cover the bowl with plastic wrap and put it in a warm place to rise for 2 to 3 hours, or until it has doubled in bulk. Punch the dough down and knead again, then divide into four pieces to make 4 loaves.

To make plaited challah with three strands:

a. Divide 1 piece of the dough into 3. Roll each piece between your palms and pull into long thin ropes about 18in (46cm) long and 1in (3cm) wide.
b. Pinch one end of all the strands together and plait them: bring the rope on the right over the middle one, then bring the one on the left over it and continue to the end.
c. Pinch the ends together and tuck them under the loaf. You may find it easier to begin plaiting in the middle of the 3 strands and plait towards

the 2 ends. Continue with the remaining 3 pieces.

5. Place the 4 loaves on well-oiled baking sheets, leaving plenty of room for them to expand, then leave to rise for 1 hour, or until doubled in bulk.

6. Now brush gently with the beaten egg yolks or if you want to sprinkle with poppy or sesame seeds, brush first with the whole beaten egg (the seeds stick better if the white is there too).

7. Bake in pre-heated 350°F (180°C) oven for 30-40 mins or until the loaves are beautifully golden-brown. They are done if they sound hollow when you tap the bottoms.

Pao de Queijo (Cheese Bread)

Origin
Brazil.

Recipe supplied by
Adriana Meirelles, Hill Street, Totterdown.

Ingredients
4 cups of sour tapioca starch flour
1 cup grated Parmesan cheese
4 eggs (unbeaten)
2 tbsp of flour
1 tsp salt
¼ cup of milk

I've chosen this recipe from my home country because it is so easy and quick to make and my neighbours in Totterdown all seem to like it.

Method
1. Combine all the ingredients in a bowl and mix.
2. Roll into small balls with a soup spoon and place on a greased oven tray.
3. Bake in a pre-heated oven at gas mark 5 for 20 mins or until they are golden brown.
4. Serve with a bit of butter. They are delicious with tea.

TOP TIP
You can find tapioca starch flour at Justino's Market – 595 Fishponds Road in Fishponds.

Deep South (of The River) Pepper Sauce

Origin
Totterdown.

Recipe supplied by
Martin Hutchinson of Margate Street,
Victoria Park.

Ingredients
3 cayenne peppers (other chilli peppers can be
substituted to adjust heat)
1 chipotle chilli (smoked jalapeno – if not available
use 1 tsp smoked paprika powder)
Juice of ½ a lime
½ red bell pepper
2 cloves garlic
½ tsp oregano
½ tsp cumin powder
½ tsp coriander powder
½ tsp sea salt
Approx 80ml organic white wine vinegar

This is a multi-purpose sauce that can be added
to salads, stir fries, casseroles etc or sprinkled
over omelettes, pizzas – anything. It was
developed by years of experimentation.

Method
1. Whizz all the ingriemts together in a
   blender or liquidizer. Use half of the vinegar to
   start with, gradually adding more to reach the
   required consistency (bit thicker than ketchup).
2. Pour into a sterilised bottle and keep for a
   week before using. This sauce gets better with
   time and keeps for ages.

B&M

Burnham & Morrill

BROWN BREAD
ORIGINAL

99%
FAT FREE
CHOLESTEROL

Boston Brown Bread (aka 'bread in a can')

Origin
New England, USA.

Recipe supplied by
Lynn Gibbons and Andy Martin of Richmond Street who have lived in Totterdown since 2006.

Ingredients
100 g (4 oz) wholemeal flour
100 g (4 oz) rye flour
175 g (6 oz) corn meal
1.5 level tsp bicarbonate soda
1.5 level tsp salt
400 ml (¾ pint) buttermilk
225 g (8 oz) black treacle
175 g (6 oz) seedless raisins (optional)

Boston brown bread is an unusual bread which has an interesting history stemming from the limited resources available in Colonial New England. Early settlers needed bread, and since they had more cornmeal and rye flour than wheat flour, the three were combined to conserve precious stores of wheat. Because ovens were not available to all colonists, the bread was cooked by steaming, instead of baking, in a cylindrical container. Metal or glass molds were used, but today it is usually steamed in a coffee can or similar tin. After the bread is steamed, it slides out, retaining the shape of the container, and is served warm. It became, along with Boston baked beans, the traditional New England Saturday-night supper.

My mother loves it – and you can still find it, ready-made in a tin, from certain supermarkets in the New England states (Connecticut, Massachusetts, Rhode Island, New Hampshire, Vermont and Maine). My brothers and I always assumed she was the only person left who actually ate this 'bread in a can', and we found it hugely amusing every time she 'opened the can'.

It's a dark and dense, but slightly sweet, bread that is best with butter, cream cheese or the traditional beans.

Method
1. Line two 450g (1lb) coffee tins or pudding basins with foil and cut foil lids for the tops. Grease the foil well.
2. Measure all the ingredients into a large bowl and stir to mix.
3. Pour into the prepared tins, cover with foil and secure with string.
4. Place the tins on a trivet in a large, deep saucepan and add boiling water to come halfway up the tins. Cover saucepan.
5. Simmer gently for 2 hours or until a skewer inserted into the centre comes out clean. Turn out on to a wire rack and cool.

TOP TIP
Best the next day! And you can use a loaf tin if baking bread in a 'regular' tin is just too weird!

Nana's chicken soup

Origin
Russia.

Recipe supplied by
Francine Russell from All About Food who lives in Arnos Street, Totterdown.

Ingredients
A whole fowl plus feet, wings and giblets (or a roasting chicken plus a chicken stock cube)
3 pints water
2 unpeeeled onions cut in 4
3 carrots scrubbed and cut into 4
3 stalks celery
A few sprigs of parsley
2 teaspoons salt
A good pinch of pepper

My Nana introduced me to cooking at an early age. She was a feisty woman who would serve up big plates of traditional Jewish fare with a side plate of guilt! God forbid you should leave anything. "Remember all those starving children" she would say, or "What's wrong with the chicken? All of a sudden you're a vegetarian?" A Jew of Russian origin she had a great love of cooking. I have very fond memories of witnessing the great creations that emerged from her steamy, sweet smelling kitchen. I still have many of her recipes and I chose a classic that is often thought of as Jewish penicillin. A cure for all physical and emotional ailments. Enjoy!

Method
1. Put the water, salt and pepper in a large stock pot, add the feet, wings, chicken, giblets and stock cube. Cover the pot and bring to the boil then uncover and skim off any foam that has formed, then add the remaining ingredients.
2. Bring back to the boil then reduce heat and cover. Simmer very gently for 3 hours.
3. Strain the soup into one bowl and keep aside the carrots for the following day.
4. Next day remove any congealed fat and return soup to the pan and heat slowly.
5. Dice the carrots and add to the soup.
6. Serve with knaidlach (matzo balls).

Five Dhal

Origin
India and Pakistan.

Recipe supplied by
Liaqat Ali Khan and Sabiha Khan,
Wells Road, Totterdown.

Ingredients
3 tbsp mung beans
3 tbsp pigeon peas
3 tbsp yellow split peas
3 tbsp green split peas
3 tbsp chick peas
Oil or ghee
Fresh red chilli or chilli powder
One large onion (finely chopped)
Two cloves of garlic (finely chopped)
Garam masala and salt

You can find this dish all over India and Pakistan, sometimes it is made as a five dhal soup (just add water), but this version is more dry and comes from the Karachi area of Pakistan. We have lived in the Totterdown area for many years and this is just one of the many recipes we regularly cook at home. The measurements in this dish are approximate. Change them to suit your taste.

Method
1. Wash the five dhal, cover in water and bring to the boil.
2. Add fresh chilli or chilli powder to the dhal to taste. Skim the surface of the water as the dhal cooks. Cooking time depends on whether you use dry or tinned dhal.
3. When the dhal is cooked, cover the saucepan and put to one side.
4. Heat the oil or ghee in a frying pan and cook the garlic and onion together. This mixture is known as Bhagar. When the onion and garlic begins to brown, add it to the dhal, stir in, cover and leave for a few minutes. Season with garam masala and serve.

MAINS

Salmon Fishcakes

Origin
Bristol.

Recipe supplied by
Holly Cadwgan of
Fitzroy Street,
Totterdown.

Ingredients
Groundnut oil
3 spring onions,
chopped
1 tsp crushed dried
chillies
1 clove garlic
½ tsp ground coriander
1 nugget ginger, grated
Zest of 1 lemon
2 skinless and boneless
salmon fillets, diced
Dark soy sauce
Thai fish sauce
275 g (medium –
large) sweet potato
^{1}/3 of a (semi-stale)
ciabatta blended or
grated into fine crumbs
1 egg

PICTURE: *Holly Cadwgan's
salmon fishcakes are a big hit
with her family.*

This recipe has been in evolution since tasting my daughter's pureed salmon and sweet potato. She also loves the mixture but without the chillies.

Method
1. Boil sweet potato for 10 mins or until soft enough for mashing. Drain and leave to stand letting as much steam release as possible. This is important to make the fishcakes firm.
2. Meanwhile, stir-fry the onion, chilli, coriander, garlic and ginger with the salmon until the fish flakes. Add the lemon zest, splash of soy sauce and splash of fish sauce. Cook for another minute, leave to cool letting steam evaporate.
3. Using a food processor or hand blender, pulse the mixture with half of the breadcrumbs and sweet potato. Alternatively, mash with a potato masher. Separate into 6 cakes.
4. Cover each one in the beaten egg and then the bread crumbs and fry in groundnut oil until golden brown. Make sure the oil is hot when you put the cakes in and keep on a medium heat.

> **TOP TIP**
> Serve with mayonnaise mixed with half the juice from the lemon on a salad with fresh coriander.

Morrocan Lamb Shanks with Cous Cous and Tzaziki

Origin
North African.

Recipe supplied by
Gary Crossan of Brendon Road who has lived in the Totterdown area since 2005.

Ingredients
Lamb shank
2 onions
Garlic
1 tin tomatoes
Turmeric
Paprika
Bay leaves
Vegetable stock
Cous cous
Sultanas
Chick peas
Dried apricots
Pine nuts
Lemon
Coriander
Yogurt and cucumber
Mint
Cumin
Salt and pepper

Method Lamb Shank
1. Pre-heat oven at 210°C.
2. Seal shank by placing in hot tray.
3. Add diced onion and garlic.
4. Add turmeric, paprika and one tin of tomatoes.
5. Add vegetable stock.
6. Add bay leaves.
7. Salt and pepper to taste.
8. Put foil over the top and braise in the oven for 3 hours at 210°C.

Method Cous Cous
1. Dice onion and sweat off with garlic, paprika and turmeric.
2. Add cous cous.
3. Add vegetable stock until cous cous is soft but not mushy.
4. Put in the oven for 5-10 mins to make fluffy.
5. Take cous cous out of the oven and stir with a fork to break up.
6. Season with salt and pepper.
7. Add apricots, chickpeas, coriander, pine nuts, lemon zest and juice.

Method Tzatziki
1. Mix yogurt with a pinch of cumin, diced cucumber (take middle out), chopped mint, lemon juice, salt and pepper.

TOP TIP
When taking shank out of the oven, make sure meat is falling off the bone.

Harvest Pie

Origin
British.

Recipe supplied by
Tina Richardson of Harrowdene Road who has lived in the Totterdown area since 2005.

Ingredients
For pastry
225 g/6 oz plain wholemeal flour
½ tsp salt
125 g/4 oz butter
3(ish) tbsp water
1 tbsp fresh rosemary, chopped

For filling
2 large onions (red or white)
4 cloves of garlic
Sufficient quantity of root vegetables to fill pie case (squash, sweet potato, carrots, pumpkin, parsnip etc)
2 tbsp oil
Freshly ground pepper
1 tbsp of fresh rosemary, chopped
About a pint of vegetable stock

I like to use seasonal vegetables, and put this together using up the bits and pieces I can find. I think the wholemeal pastry, rosemary and root vegetables go really well together. This is a wholesome, nourishing and comforting meal.

Method
1. Chop onions and root vegetables into approximately 1 inch x 1 inch chunks. Quarter the garlic cloves and mix together. Roast in oven covered in oil at 200°C or gas mark 6.
2. Sift flour and salt (mix bran back in after sifting).
3. Rub butter into flour with fingertips until it looks like fine breadcrumbs. Then mix in rosemary.
4. Add water gradually until it forms a dough.
5. Knead on a lightly floured surface for a couple of minutes.
6. Roll out to line a greased pie tin and make pie topping.
7. Put roast vegetables into pastry case.
8. Add pepper and rosemary to stock/gravy and pour over vegetables.
9. Put pie topping over, pinch the edges together and use a small amount of gravy or stock to glaze the top of the pie.
10. Bake in a hot oven 200-220°C or gas mark 6-7.

TOP TIP
Good with mashed potato.

Ackee and Saltfish, BS3 Style

Origin
Jamaica.

Recipe supplied by
Bugsy from The Oxford pub, Oxford Street, who has lived in Totterdown all his life.

Ingredients
Scallions – bunch of big spring onions
2 large onions
Fresh thyme
1-2 tins ackee – you can find it in West Indian shops in Easton
Rice
Scotch bonnet/chilli – be careful!
4 large tomatoes, quartered
Cod
Black pepper and salt to season
Corn oil (or butter or olive oil)

Salt fish is basically cod, which is a cold-water fish. It is unusual that it is a Jamaican national dish because the fish is imported from the UK. In Jamaica, you can get parrot fish and red snapper but they choose a cold-water fish as a national dish!

Method
1. Soak the cod for 24 hours in cold water to dilute the salt or boil to get rid of the salt. If cod has skin, de-bone or remove skin to taste.
2. Sweat onions in corn oil, olive oil or butter.
3. Add seasoning and tomatoes.
4. Add cod to the rest of the ingredients.
5. Add ackee (1-2 tins) and heat thoroughly. Be careful not to stir too much to avoid breaking the ackee.
6. Serve with plain rice, or alternatively rice and peas, plantain, yam or boiled dumplings.

PICTURE: *Bugsy at the Oxford.*

TOP TIP
You can add green peppers if you like, but I don't like them! I use butter or olive oil to sweat onions. You can add prawns and lobster to this dish.

JPS Corned Beef Hash

Origin
British.

Recipe supplied by
Johnston, Phil and Sam from Kensal Avenue, Windmill Hill. They have lived in the Totterdown area since 2002.

Ingredients
1 large onion
1 big tin corned beef
3 large potatoes
1 tin tomatoes
A mixture of crushed cornflakes and grated cheese (enough to cover dish well)
Mixed herbs
White pepper
Worcestershire sauce

Once upon a time Johnston and Phil were watching GMTV when the programme started talking about the war. This led them to think about what people living in the war might eat. So they started coming up with different ideas for wartime recipes and corned beef hash seemed like the best idea. Suddenly, there was a rumble and their neighbour Sam burst through the door with some more ideas for the recipe. Their ideas joined forces and that is how 'JPS' corned beef hash was born.

Method
1. Dice onion and chop potatoes into cubes.
2. Fry onions and potatoes until onion browns.
3. Add tin of tomatoes, herbs, Worcestershire sauce, pepper and salt.
4. Cover and simmer for 15 mins.
5. Chop corned beef into 2cm cubes and add. Simmer for a further 5 mins.
6. Mix cornflakes with cheese.
7. Remove corned beef mix from heat and cover with cornflakes and cheese. Place in ovenproof dish and grill until golden brown.

PICTURE: *Johnston, Phil and Sam capture the VE Day spirit with their corned beef hash.*

TOP TIP
Serve with crusty organic bread and a rustic mixed leaf salad with croutons and balsamic dressing.

Simple Spring Spaghetti

Origin
Totteralian.

Recipe supplied by
Nicky and Nathan of
Oxford Street.
Totterdown. residents
since 2006.

Ingredients
Spaghetti – decent
portion for 2 people,
150-200 g, the longer
the better
1 lemon
Pine nuts – a generous
handful
Asparagus – about 6
spears
Balsamic vinegar
Original olive oil with a
good flavour
Sea salt – a soft kind
like Maldon
8 -10 fresh basil leaves

I'm sure the original pasta recipe has been cooked in Italy for centuries but I was still impressed when Nathan cooked it for me and served it on one big plate with two forks! It became a firm favourite and we experimented with extra ingredients until we found local British asparagus to be the best. It's such a quick and yummy recipe that we find ourselves eating it at least once a week in spring. It tastes especially good with a glass of white wine.

Method
1. Put the spaghetti on to boil whilst gently toasting the pine nuts in a dry heavy-based pan until lightly browned.
2. Chop the asparagus into large chunks and stir into a bowl containing a generous slug of balsamic vinegar, a little olive oil and a good pinch of salt. Make sure the asparagus is coated and place on a ridged grill pan over a high heat. Grill the spears for 3-4 minutes moving them around the pan.
3. Drain the pasta and return to the pan with a glug of olive oil, the toasted pine nuts and grilled asparagus.
4. Squeeze most of the lemon into the pan and tear up the fresh basil leaves.
5. Stir it once more and serve (on one plate or two) with some grated parmesan and black pepper if desired.

TOP TIP
There are many additions to this – sun-dried tomatoes or Parma ham work especially well.

Mock Chopped 'Liver'

Origin
Bristolian/Jewish.

Recipe supplied by
Naomi Berry of Oxford Street, Totterdown.

Ingredients
6 oz roughly ground walnuts (don't buy ready ground, get them whole and lightly roast/toast to bring out flavour, then mash them up)
2 or 3 large hard-boiled eggs
1 very large onion, finely chopped
1 lb frozen runner or green beans (you can use fresh but will need to steam to soften before using)
Oil (can be olive but no real need as sunflower or vegetable oil is fine too)
Salt

Serves two greedies.
Preparation time: 5 mins.
Cooking time: 15 mins.

My lovely granny used to make this superb low-fat version of a Jewish staple. It tastes surprisingly meaty and will satisfy the most carnivorous of carnivores. It is delicious served in a big bowl with toasted granary bread and a peppery green salad.

Method
1. Cook beans.
2. Boil eggs (leave in cold water for a few minutes to make peeling easier).
3. Sauté onion gently for quite a while (at least 10 mins) allowing bits to go brown and caramelise. This is what adds the meaty flavour so spend the time to do this slooooowly.
4. Combine beans, eggs, hot onion mixture and walnuts and season with quite a liberal dose of salt.
5. Blend/liquidise everything to desired consistency.

TOP TIP
If mixture is a bit too wet add some sautéed mushrooms to thicken. If mixture is too dry, try adding a drop of olive oil and stock.

Greek Pizza with Spinich, Feta and Rosemary

Origin
Greek.

Recipe supplied by
Naomi Berry of Oxford Street, Totterdown.

Ingredients
Pizza dough (you can get great ready made packets which you just add water and knead)
1 tbsp olive oil
1 medium red onion, chopped
2 garlic cloves, chopped
1 bag of spinach
1 tsp chopped lemon zest
Handful of black olives de-stoned and roughly chopped
3 oz feta
¼ lb grated mozzarella
½ oz parmesan
1 tsp fresh rosemary, finely chopped

Serves two.
Preparation time: 15 minutes.
Cooking time: 12 minutes.

Method
1. Make up dough.
2. Get oven hot, hot, hot.
3. Heat oil and sauté onion until tender with salt and pepper.
4. Add 1 clove of garlic to onions and cook for a further minute (don't let garlic catch or go brown as this tastes icky).
5. Scoop this mixture out into bowl and set aside.
6. Using same pan, heat a little more oil and wilt spinach with a bit more salt and pepper and remaining garlic. Keep the spinach green by doing this quickly.
7. Drain spinach and give a good hard squeeze to remove all excess liquid, then chop up along with lemon zest.
8. Now you're ready to start assembling the pizza. Rub a little oil (or tomato puree) on pizza base then layer up onion mixture, spinach, olives, feta and mozzarella.
9. Bake according to dough instructions (normally around 8-12 minutes) and then sprinkle with rosemary and parmesan just before serving.

Smoked Cod and Leek Lasagne

Origin
Italy.

Recipe supplied by
Charles Hutchings of Hill Street, who has lived in Totterdown since 2006.

Ingredients
500 g smoked cod loin
600 ml semi-skimmed milk
50 g butter
40 g plain flour
Some fresh parsley, roughly chopped
Salt and pepper
400 g leeks, sliced
4 fresh or 6 dried lasagne sheets (depending on size of your dish)
25 g mature cheddar cheese, grated

Serves four people.
Preparation time: 15 mins.
Cooking time: 30 mins.

An easy recipe that I think originally came from a supermarket. Most of our family and friends have sampled it at least once in the last few years and have always left clean plates!

Method
1. Pre-heat oven to 200°C/400°F, gas mark 6.
2. Place cod loin in large saucepan with the milk. Bring to boil and simmer gently for 5 minutes until the fish is just cooked. Remove the fish, flake and set aside (check for bones). Reserve the milk.
3. Cook the leeks for 5 minutes on a moderate heat in 10g of butter, stirring occasionally until softened.
4. Meanwhile, melt 40g butter in a pan, stir in flour and cook for 1 minute, stirring continuously. Gradually whisk in the reserved milk, bring to boil and simmer for 4-5 minutes, stirring constantly until thickened. Remove from heat, add cod and parsley. Season.
5. Place half the fish mixture in the base of a lightly buttered ovenproof dish. Top with half the lasagne sheets, then half the remaining fish mixture, half the leeks and the remaining lasagne sheets. Spoon over remaining leeks and fish mixture. Sprinkle cheese on top and bake in the pre-heated oven for 20 mins until cooked through and golden.
6. Serve with a salad.

PICTURE: *Charles Hutchings prepares his Smoked Cod and Leek Lasagne at his home in Hill Street.*

Middle Eastern Mezze

Origin
Middle East.

Recipe supplied by
Cath Greig of Vale Street, resident of Totterdown since 1992.

My family are Armenian and some of their favourite recipes are ones that appear in many of the Middle Eastern cultures. One is mezze – their version of hors d'ouvres. My aunt, Alice Peltegian, is the best cook in our family and she has passed some of her tried and tested recipes to me. Like many cultures, recipes are handed down through the experience of cooking rather than through a written down recipe and can often be adapted according to the cook's taste. Many of the dishes are quite labour intensive and the opposite of fast food. With the following dishes, I've had the same experience. I don't refer to a recipe but I've worked out ingredient quantities so that other people can give it a go. I have found that the mezze dishes that can be bought in cafés/restaurants as part of tapas plates are pale imitations of the home-cooked versions.

Dolmades *(Stuffed vine leaves)*
Ingredients
Vine leaves: either pre-packaged in brine or fresh if you have a broad leaved vine in your garden/allotment
Rice stuffing (to be prepared the day before needed)
1 cup of pudding rice
2 cups of onions, chopped
1 cup of olive oil
1 or 2 ripe fresh tomatoes, roughly chopped
1 red pepper, finely chopped
2 tbsp of parsley finely chopped
2 tbsp dried mint
Peel of one lemon
1-2 lemons, freshly squeezed
¼ tsp of paprika
¼ tsp of cinnamon

(continues overleaf)

Middle Eastern Mezze (continued from p55)

Method

1. Put oil in a large pan. As it heats up, add all ingredients except vine leaves. Warm together on a low heat and stir. Then put aside to use the next day to give time for the mixture to absorb the juices and the flavours to infuse.

2. Stuffing the vine leaves: vine leaves packaged with brine can be obtained from delis and local shops like Patco's or further afield at the Sweet Mart in Easton. If you have a vine in your garden you can use the fresh leaves from that. If pre-packaged, follow the instructions on the pack. If using fresh leaves – choose undamaged broad leaves and plunge a few at a time into boiling water until they change to a darker green colour. To stuff, lay out a vine leaf vein side upwards with the pointed end facing away from you. Put about a teaspoon of rice mix in the centre and fold the end of the vine leaf that's nearest to you over the rice mix, then fold the sides of the leaf in and finish by rolling up into a cigar shape. The more you do the easier it gets!

3. Line a heavy-bottomed pan with damaged leaves and then carefully put the rolled up vine leaves into the pan. Lay a plate on top to stop them unravelling. Add water to the pan so that it comes above the level of the plate. Add ¼ pint of olive oil, a pinch of salt and the juice of a lemon. Put the lid on the pan and simmer for 45 – 60 mins. Add water if necessary.

The dolmades are best served at room temperature. If you have stuffing left over you can use it to stuff tomatoes, peppers or cabbage leaves.

Baba Ganoush *(Aubergine dip)*

Ingredients

2 medium-sized aubergines
1 clove of garlic
4 tbsp of tahini (or more to taste)
Juice of one lemon
1 tsp salt

Method

1. Pre-heat the grill and prepare the aubergines by pricking them all over with a fork and then putting them onto a foil-lined grill pan and place under the grill. As the skin on the aubergines becomes charred, turn them a little way until gradually the whole skin becomes charred and the insides have become soft. Leave to cool.

2. When cool enough to handle, peel away the charred skin and put the flesh into a sieve. Place a plate and heavy weight on top of the flesh so that its juices drain off. Most recipes don't include this step but I find that by draining the liquid, the Baba Ganoush has a much finer flavour. I tend to do this overnight but it could be left for 3 – 4 hours.

3. Once the flesh has been drained of liquid, put

all the ingredients in a blender or food processor and combine until smooth. Taste and add more tahini/lemon juice/garlic according to preference. This can be prepared by hand by chopping the aubergine flesh and then mixing the other ingredients in with a fork.

4. Serve cold or at room temperature with pitta bread, vegetable crudités etc.

Tabbouleh *(Bulgar wheat salad)*
Ingredients
4 oz/125 g of fine bulgar wheat (available from Patco's and delis)

2 ripe tomatoes

¼ cucumber

5-6 spring onions, finely chopped

A large bunch of parsley – the Banana Boat sells large bunches – supermarkets tend to sell tiny packaged amounts – try and get at least

4 oz/125 g

Juice of 2 lemons

1 tsp salt

2 tbsp olive oil

2-3 tbsp tahini

1 tbsp tomato puree

Method

1. Wash, drain and dry the bulgar thoroughly. Put into a large bowl. If you have a food processor, put the tomatoes and cucumber into the bowl and puree them before adding to the bulgar. Use the food processor to chop the parsley finely before also adding to the bulgar. If you don't have a food processor, just chop tomatoes, cucumber and parsley by hand with a sharp knife.

2. Add the rest of the ingredients to the bulgar mix and combine thoroughly. It's best to leave this mixture overnight to allow the bulgar to soak up the juices of the pureed vegetables, lemon juice etc.

3. Before serving, taste the tabbouleh and add anything that you feel it might lack. I love lemon juice so tend to be a bit more lavish with that!

TOP TIP

Try to make things a day ahead as the food can taste so much better once all the flavours have infused and been absorbed.

..icken Paella

Origin
Spain.

Recipe supplied by
Windmill Hill
City Farm.

This dish comes from Valencia on the east coast of Spain. The land is flat and the weather conditions are perfect for growing rice. Paella was first created by families that didn't have any money and had to use the basic ingredients that grew around them. You'll be surprised to know that wild rats were once used instead of chickens for paella, because the rice fields were infested with them.

Ingredients
1 chicken, jointed, cut into bite-sized pieces
1 tbsp fresh rosemary, or to taste
100 ml olive oil
3 chopped tomatoes
½ red pepper, diced
2 garlic cloves, finely chopped
2 fresh bay leaves
500 ml water, approximate quantity
A good pinch saffron strands
300 g Spanish paella rice
75 g runner beans, washed and chopped
2 globe artichokes, peeled and sliced
75 g butter beans, cooked
Lemon, to serve

Method
1. You will need a pan, preferably a paella pan or very large frying pan.
2. Heat the olive oil in a large pan and fry the garlic and chopped rosemary over a moderate heat, until browned.
3. Add the tomatoes, red pepper, runner beans, artichokes and butter beans. Fry until vegetables start browning.
4. Add the chicken pieces and fry until the surface of the meat is coloured all over.
5. Add the water and bay leaves and simmer for about 20 mins on a low heat.
6. Add the rice to the pan and continue cooking on a low heat for 15 mins. The characteristic yellow colour of paella is brought by saffron added to the boiling rice. Saffron is very expensive, so you can use colorants or turmeric to achieve the same effect. You might need to add a little more water if it evaporates before the rice has cooked. The rice at this stage shouldn't be tender – it should still have a bite to it.
7. If you prefer to use shellfish like squid, tiger prawns and mussels in this dish, add them with the chicken in stage 4 or substitute the meat completely by the shellfish.
8. Cut lemon wedges, place them around the pan, bring the pan to the table and let everyone help themselves.

PICTURE: *Roz Newman (left) and Maria Bernguer at the Windmill Hill City Farm Café.*

Delhi Rajna

Origin
Delhi.

Recipe supplied by
Panna Patel from
Patco, Wells Road,
Totterdown.

Ingredients
1 tin red kidney beans
2 onions
1 tomato
A good pinch of dried
garlic, ginger, chilli,
coriander powder,
garam masala,
turmeric, salt
1 tsp tomato puree

This is very quick to prepare and a good healthy option. It is a very popular dish in India. Use a good pinch of the spices to start with and then vary to suit your taste.

Method
Fry onions in pan, add chopped tomato, garlic, ginger, chilli, 1 tsp of tomato puree, coriander powder, salt, turmeric, and garam masala, mix well. Add kidney beans. Garnish with fresh coriander. Serve with naan, pitta bread, partha or rice.

Chicory and Ham Gratin

Origin
France.

Recipe supplied by
Steph Stephens of Pylle Hill Crescent who
has lived in the Totterdown area on and off
since 2002 .

Ingredients
8-10 chicories (2 or 3 per person)
Sliced ham (not smoked)
Grated cheese (Emmental, Gruyère or Cheddar)
Vinegar

Serves four.

As far as I know, this recipe has been used in
France for many generations. Chicory is much
more mainstream in France than it is here. It is
nice cooked in a béchamel sauce or raw and
chopped in a vinaigrette dressing. It was a
favourite of mine when my mum was making it in
France. It is now in high demand from my
husband and three children.

Method
1. Pre-heat the oven at 220°C or gas mark 7.
2. Boil the chicory and drain (it is very watery so
   leave to drain for a while or squeeze).
3. Butter an oven-proof dish and spread the
   bottom with slices of ham.
4. Add a layer of a third of the cheese.
5. Spread the chicory on top.
6. Cover the chicory with another third of the
   cheese.
7. Add a layer of ham.
8. Sprinkle the rest of the cheese on top.
9. Cook in the oven for 30 mins until brown. Add
   vinegar once served.

TOP TIP
Because it is French, alcohol vinegar (impossible to find in Britain) and Gruyère or Emmental should
be used but you can adapt to your taste. We use Cheddar (when in Rome and all that). Some
people add vinegar before cooking but most prefer to add it when it is served. You can also
substitute this with lemon juice.

chicken Tagine

Origin
North Africa.

Recipe supplied by
Bart Spices, York Road, Totterdown.

Ingredients
1 large chopped onion
3 tbsp oil
4 chicken breasts
4 tsp Bart Ras El Hanout
1 tsp Bart Garlic in sunflower oil
1 tsp Bart Ginger in sunflower oil
The peel of one lemon
125 g pitted green olives
Salt and pepper to taste
Chicken stock
3 tsp Bart Coriander in sunflower oil
Cous cous to serve

Established in Bristol in the 1960s, Bart Spices continues to be a growing independent food company, whose heart and soul is in supplying only the very finest quality food ingredients from around the globe. Our passion for offering the most wonderful range of herbs, spices and coconut products allows you to recreate and enjoy wonderful dishes from every corner of the world in your own home.

Method
1. Soften the onion in oil. Add the chicken breasts and cook for 2 minutes.
2. Stir in the Ras El Hanout, garlic, ginger, lemon peel and green olives. Add salt and pepper to taste.
3. Add enough chicken stock to just cover the chicken and bring to the boil.
4. Cover and simmer for 35 mins. Stir in the coriander.
5. Serve with cous cous.

Kipper Kedgeree

Origin
British Raj.

Recipe supplied by
Vishnu who has lived in Totterdown since the late 1970s among a large Asian Christian family dotted around the area.

Ingredients
½ cup of sunflower oil
1 onion, chopped
1 tin of chopped tomatoes
1 tbsp salt
2 cloves garlic, chopped
Handful of coriander, chopped
4 boiled eggs, sliced
5 fillets of smoked kippers
4 cups of basmati rice

Serves 4.

This dish was originally called Kicharee and originates from India – it consists of rice and lentils. In the days of the British Raj in India, this dish was incorporated with eggs and kippers which then the British ate for breakfast. So realistically, they are two separate dishes.

Method
1. Start by browning the chopped onions in the sunflower oil.
2. Add the chopped tomatoes, salt and the garlic. Cook for 2 mins and then add the chopped coriander.
3. Soak the rice until each grain becomes fully white and the starch is drained.
4. Boil the rice for 20 mins with water an inch higher than the rice.
5. Cook the smoked kippers and then mash them up and mix with all the other ingredients and add to the rice.
6. Garnish with a few sliced up hard-boiled eggs.

Rabbit Stew

My grandmother used to cook this when I visited her in Norfolk. This is quite a light stew cooked in the pot.

Origin
Norfolk.

Recipe supplied by
Rob Hardy of Balmain Street who has lived in Totterdown since 2002.

Ingredients
1 rabbit (in 4 joints)
1 medium onion
1 clove garlic
2 medium leeks
4 carrots
Salt and pepper to season
Fresh herbs
Water
White wine or dry cider (optional)

Method
1. Poach the rabbit in a large pan with a little water for about 25 mins or until meat becomes tender. Keep adding water if it starts to dry up.
2. Roughly chop the vegetables and add to pot. Season to taste.
3. Add enough water to cover and cook for a further 20-30 mins.
4. When the carrot is cooked, add herbs and turn the heat down.
5. Add a splash of dry cider or wine vinegar if you like.
6. Simmer on low heat for 10 mins to reduce the liquid slightly and allow flavours to develop.
7. Season and serve with mashed potato.

..ney Bean Kiev

Origin
Totterdown.

Recipe supplied by
Emma and Warwick at the Shakespeare pub, Henry Street, Totterdown.

Ingredients
Garlic butter
100 g butter
3 garlic cloves
1 tbsp chopped parsley

Bean patties
650 g canned red kidney beans
150 g fresh breadcrumbs (brown or white)
25 g butter
1 leek, chopped
1 celery stick, chopped
1 tbsp parsley, chopped
1 egg, beaten
Salt and pepper to season
Vegetable oil for shallow frying

This is available as a vegetarian option on the Shakey Sunday lunch menu.

Method
1. To make garlic butter, blend butter, garlic and parsley together. Roll the mixture into a sausage shape and place in the fridge to chill.
2. Using potato masher, mash the kidney beans in a mixing bowl and stir in 75g of breadcrumbs until thoroughly blended.
3. Melt the butter in a pan and sauté the leeks and celery for 3-4 mins.
4. Add the beans to the pan together with the parsley, season with salt and pepper and mix well. Remove from the heat and allow to cool slightly.
5. Shape the bean mixture into four equal size ovals.
6. Slice the garlic butter into four and place a slice into each bean patty. Mould the patty around the garlic butter.
7. Dip each patty into the beaten egg and coat in breadcrumbs.
8. Heat a little oil in a frying pan and fry the patties for 8-10 mins until golden.
9. Serve and enjoy.

PICTURE: *Warwick and Emma (right) with son Harvey and Rhiannon at the Shakespeare.*

TOP TIP
You can vary this recipe by using mozzarella and chopped chillies instead of garlic butter.

184c Wells rd, Knowle BS4 2AL 0117 971 3377 www.acappellas.co.uk

OPEN

WiFi

Pop in fill up

venue

Heavy Metal!

Acappella

Spring Lamb and Feta Burger

Origin
Australia.

Recipe supplied by
Paul Stewart of
A cappella on Wells
Road who is from
Australia. He has been
working in Totterdown
since 2006.

Ingredients
500 g minced lamb
125 g feta cheese
Handful of pine nuts
1 red onion, diced
Breadcrumbs (2 slices)
Handful of raisins (or
sultanas)
Sprig of rosemary,
finely chopped
Salt and pepper (to
season)
1 egg

Serves four.

I grew up in Australia, so I've been to and hosted many a BBQ. They are a great chance to relax with friends and eat good food. Everybody brings a dish and competition is tough in the burger stakes. This crowd-pleasing recipe is influenced by Melbourne's Greek community (second largest outside Athens) and is guaranteed to be the most bonza burger of any BBQ.

Method

1. Sprinkle a handful of pine nuts onto a roasting tray and place under the grill. Keep watch over them as they burn easily. When they start to go golden, remove, put to one side and allow to cool.
2. Place two slices of bread into a food processor and blitz to make breadcrumbs. Put to one side.
3. Remove the rosemary leaves from the stalks and chop finely.
4. Dice the red onion.
5. Grab a large mixing bowl and add your minced lamb, then crumble the feta into small pieces and add to the lamb. Add all of the remaining ingredients. Now it's time to get stuck in. With your hands, mix together all the ingredients. Take a healthy handful of the mixture and pat firmly between the palms of your hands until you have a solid burger about 2cm thick. You should have enough for 4 to 5 burgers.
6. If the mixture isn't binding, you can add the yolk of another egg. If it's too soggy add some more breadcrumbs.
7. Place your burgers on a tray, cover with cling film and refrigerate for 2 hours before cooking. These burgers also freeze well.
8. Cook gently for 4-5 mins per side on the BBQ. If it's not BBQ weather, don't sweat it! Cook them in a frying pan on a low to medium heat.

> **TOP TIP**
> We serve these in A cappella on top of grilled ciabatta with garlic mayonnaise, spinach and cherry tomato salad. Keep your flavours simple though because the burger is packed with flavour.

12-hour Braised Shoulder of Lamb

Origin
France.

Recipe supplied by
Tim Owen of Stanley Hill who has lived in Totterdown since 1991.

Ingredients
1 shoulder of lamb (salt marsh lamb is preferable and available from Taste on the A38)
Sprigs of parsley, thyme, rosemary and 2 bay leaves (fresh have better flavour)
1 bottle of cabernet sauvignon
5 shallots, peeled and roughly chopped
1 leek
2 sticks of celery
2 carrots
1 whole head of garlic, cut into two horizontally
Couple of lugs of balsamic vinegar
Maldon sea salt
Freshly-milled black pepper

Serves six to eight.

PICTURE: *Tim Owen serves his lamb dish and then takes a picture of it on his mobile phone.*

This recipe came from my brain. It's nothing clever, just classic French cooking. I cooked it for four other fellow roofers and one of them (a 16-stone macho man) was almost reduced to tears when he tasted the combination of flavours. Please try cooking this – you'll feel like Marco Pierre White.

Method
1. Brown lamb on all sides in a large Le Creuset-style casserole pan and remove to one side.
2. Place all vegetables and herbs in the pan and allow to soften a little in the lamby olive oil.
3. Add lamb back to pan and cover with the wine and vinegar (if liquid does not cover lamb, then do so with water). Season lightly with salt and pepper – you can always check seasoning at the end.
4. Cook on the lowest possible setting for your oven for 8-12 hours (preferably 12 or this recipe would have to be re-named).
5. Carefully remove lamb from the pan because it will be collapsing at this point and put in a low oven to keep warm. Pass vegetables and liquid through a sieve making sure you squeeze out every last bit of flavour.

TOP TIP
Don't be afraid to cook for the full 12 hours. The lamb can not dry out due to the high fat content.

6. Put liquid back in cleaned pan and reduce on the highest heat until you are left with a fantastic gravy-like consistency (it should be dark and ridiculously flavoursome). At this stage or at the pre-reduction stage, you may want to skim off some of the fat but I don't bother.

7. Check seasoning of your gravy and your lamb. Flake lamb off the bone and serve with dauphinoise or boulangerie potatoes and a lovely big spoonful of salsa verde, oh, and the stupendous gravy.

Killer Beef Burger...
with an Italian Twist

Origin
Totterdown.

Recipe supplied by
Eamon Fullalove from
the Star and Dove,
St Luke's Road,
Totterdown.

Killer beef burger
Ingredients
Ground beef – 200 g
per person
1 decent-sized onion
2 gloves garlic
3 rashers of decent dry
cured bacon/or
pancetta
1 tbsp fennel seeds
2 bay leaves
1 tbsp salt
A pinch of dried chilli
Olive oil
1 tsp of nutmeg, grated
50 g of best parmesan,
grated
A bunch of tarragon,
chopped finely
A handful of parsley,
chopped

Method
1. Take the onion and chop it finely and add to the garlic (crushed with the side of a knife).
2. Then take the bacon, cut into little pieces or even better use pancetta.
3. Put the chopped bacon, onion and garlic in a frying pan with the sea salt, fennel seeds, bay leaves and dried chilli.
4. Add a splash of olive oil and put on a gentle heat and cook it all SLOWLY without adding colour to the onions.
5. Take it off the heat and put it next to a window to cool down. Take out the bay leaves.
6. Grate the nutmeg into the mix and add the parmesan. You can use the dust-like stuff that smells of vomit... upon your head be it.
7. Add the tarragon and chopped parsley.
8. Put the mix in a bowl with your ground beef and give it a good old mix, then take a small piece of mix and form it into a little disc about the size of a two pound coin...
9. Fry this off on both sides and eat it to test if you have added enough seasoning. If all is good, shape the mix into roughly 200g balls and then flatten them out into burger-like discs.
10. Put them in the fridge for an hour so they won't set fire to your barbie when you cook them.
11. Serve 'em up in a nice toasted bun with a salad and a good whack of home-made ketchup (opposite) and enjoy!!

PICTURE: *Staff at the Star and Dove look forward to Eamon's Killer Burgers.*

Home-grown tomato ketchup
Ingredients
Four cans of tinned tomatoes
Juice of one orange
Two cinnamon sticks
A block of tamarind about half the size of a bar
of soap

Method
1. Put tinned tomatoes in a saucepan with the
   orange juice, cinnamon sticks and tamarind.
2. Cook all this down for about two hours on a
   really low heat until it all goes sticky and thick.
3. Pass it through a sieve and add a bit of salt
   and pepper if needed.

Roast Chicken, Bacon and Leeks with a Cream of White Wine and Tarragon Sauce

Origin
Irish.

Recipe supplied by
Sharman Chater of William Street who moved to Totterdown in 2008.

Ingredients
1 tbsp vegetable oil
2 tbsp unsalted butter
3-3.5 lb/1.5 kg chicken
8 oz/225 g unsmoked streaky bacon
1 lb/450 g leeks
4-6 whole cloves of garlic
A good glug of dry white wine
½ cup chicken stock
8 fl oz/1 cup double cream
1 heaped tbsp chopped fresh or dried tarragon
Freshly ground black pepper (no salt required)

Serves four to six.

I'm not Irish and unfortunately I've never been to Ireland, but this simple and true Irish dish is just wonderful. I've cooked it for all my family and they all love it too. It's so hearty and substantial.

Method
1. Pre-heat the oven to 180°C/gas mark 4.
2. Wash the chicken inside and out and pat it dry with kitchen paper.
3. Heat the oil in a large, flame-proof casserole dish. Add the chicken and cook, breast-side down for 5 mins until golden. Add the butter for the last couple of minutes.
4. Remove the chicken from the casserole dish and set aside.
5. Roughly chop the bacon and add to the casserole. Fry for 5 mins until golden.
6. Top and tail the leeks, cut them into 1-inch pieces and add to the dish. Cook for a further 5 mins.
7. Place the chicken, breast side up, on top of the leeks and bacon. Add the garlic cloves and the wine. Cover and cook in the oven for 1 hour. Remove the lid and cook for a further 30 mins to crisp the skin.
8. Remove the chicken, bacon, garlic and leeks and keep warm. Skim the fat from the juices, then add the stock and the cream and bring to the boil. Cook for 5 mins, until slightly reduced and thickened. Stir in the tarragon. Add pepper to taste.
9. Carve the chicken and serve with the bacon, leeks and delicious sauce.

TOP TIP
Boiled potatoes and steamed spring greens are traditional to Irish cooking and accompany this dish well. As does a nice cold glass of Guinness. Enjoy!

...en Tikka Masala

Origin
India.

Recipe supplied by
Best Spice, Wells Road, Totterdown.

Ingredients
2 tbsp coriander seeds
2 tbsp paprika
2 tbsp jeera
1 tsp mango powder
1 tsp chilli power
Juice of one lime
10 tsp good thick yoghurt
Salt to taste
2 lb chicken, diced
5 to 6 gloves garlic, chopped
Chicken stock or water
Oil

Mr Meah, the head chef, has been cooking Indian food since 1992. He began his career in London, winning several awards. He then decided to move to Bristol and set up a take-away in a multi-cultural area where people from different walks of life can enjoy traditional tikka masala.

Method
1. Grind the spices and mix with yoghurt to make the marinade.
2. Marinade chicken in fridge for 24 hours.
3. Heat the oil in frying pan or wok until very hot.
4. Stir fry chicken vigorously for about 5 mins.
5. Take out chicken and keep warm.
6. Fry the onion and garlic until just browning and return chicken with any remaining marinade, plus the stock, plus more spices if you think the sauce needs it – an extra tsp of cumin and coriander may 'lift' it a little.
7. Simmer until the chicken is cooked and the sauce is nice and thick. Serve.

PICTURE: *In the kitchen at Best Spice on Wells Road.*

aleem (Lamb and Dhal curry)

Origin
India and Pakistan.

Recipe supplied by
Liaqat Ali Khan and Sabiha Khan, Wells Road, Totterdown.

Ingredients
3 tbsp moong dahl
3 tbsp masoor dahl (red lentils)
3 tbsp chana dahl
3 tbsp barley
3 tbsp rice
1 lb lamb or mutton, minced or cubed
1 fresh red chilli or chilli powder (to taste)
Turmeric, ginger and cumin
2 cloves of garlic, finely chopped
1 large onion, chopped
Lemon juice
Garam masala

We never follow a recipe, so I hope the quantities we've given are correct! Haleem is usually made with lamb, but you could use chicken or beef.

Method
1. Put the dhal, rice and barley in a pan, bring to the boil and simmer for two hours until cooked.
2. Add half the garlic, ginger, salt, chilli and turmeric to the dhal while it is simmering.
3. In a separate pan cook the meat thoroughly with the remaining garlic, ginger, salt, chilli and turmeric. When cooked add to the dahl and cook for a further 10 minutes, seasoning with cumin.
4. Place in separate side dishes. Season with lemon juice and garam masala.

TOP TIP
This dish is often served with salads – finely chopped mint, fresh coriander and green chilli.

Chicken Fricasee

Origin
Jamaica.

Recipe supplied by
Dorell and Elaine Parker, Hill Street, Totterdown.

Ingredients
1 chicken (2 kg/4.5 lb) or 6-8 chicken pieces
Lemon juice
Salt
3 tbsp ground black pepper
2 cloves garlic, crushed
2 onions, sliced
1 red chilli pepper, chopped
50 ml cooking oil
500-700 ml warm water
1 sprig of fresh or sprinkle of dried thyme
1 sprig of fresh or sprinkle of dried rosemary

We came to Bristol from Jamaica in 1960 and we've lived happily in Totterdown since 1972. We selected this recipe because it is one of our favourite traditional Jamaican recipes. This dish is usually served on Sundays and special occasions along with another traditional Jamaican dish called Rice and Peas.

Method
1. Wash the chicken and rub over with lemon juice.
2. Cut into joints and place in a large bowl. Season with salt, three tablespoons of black pepper and add the rest of the seasoning. Rub the seasoning into the chicken and leave to marinate for 15 mins.
3. Put the cooking oil into the frying pan. When hot, shake the seasoning from the chicken pieces and place them in the frying pan. When the chicken is very brown remove from the frying pan. Remove the frying pan from the cooker.
4. Lower the heat and put the frying pan back on the cooker. Place seasoning in the frying pan, add the warm water, bring to the boil and add the chicken. Cover the frying pan and simmer for one hour or until the chicken is tender.
5. Taste the juices for salt. If the gravy is too runny, reduce it by increasing the heat and leaving the cover off until the excess liquid evaporates. The juices from the chicken along with the seasoning will provide a thick gravy. Serve with rice and peas or white rice.

Geordie Tatie Dauph

V

Origin
Newcastle.

Recipe supplied by
Geordie Johnnie of
Cemetery Road,
Totterdown.

Ingredients
1 lb taties – Maris
Pipers or any other
fleshy whites
1 pint good chicken or
veg stock
500 ml single cream –
make sure it's a good
cream or it will
separate too easily
200 ml sour cream
100 g ricotta
(mascarpone will do at
a push)
Bunch of fresh chives
2 tbsp olive oil
2 cloves garlic
Salt and pepper

Serves four.

I would love to spread the news about some of my food. I'm not a chef but
cook for my friends a lot. I'm from Newcastle originally so my food is often
warming stuff rather than faffy salads! This is a warming and calorie-heavy
version of the original.

Method
1. Pre-heat the oven to about 220°C or equivalent.
2. Brush a medium-sized ceramic lasagne dish with all the oil.
3. Cut each clove of garlic in half and squeeze all four halves around the
   sides and base of the dish (leave the cloves in the bottom for an extra
   wee kick!).
4. Slice all the potatoes into about 10p thick slices. Discard the pointy ends
   as they'll cook too quickly and go mushy.
5. Put enough of the stock into the dish to cover the base then lay out a layer
   of potato slices. Cover with a splash more stock, a splash of single cream
   and three blobs of sour cream, spaced out evenly plus a pinch of salt and
   pepper.
6. Repeat layers until 1 inch from the top of the dish. Top with the remaining
   cream, sour cream, chives, and ricotta/mascarpone.
7. Put the dish in the oven for at least 1 hour at 200-220°C. Turn down to
   120°C-ish after 1 hour and serve when ready – yumzoid!

PICTURE: Geordie Johnnie displays his favourite dish from the North East.

ndmill Sausage Stew

Origin
Greek.

Recipe supplied by
Matt Lepper of the Windmill pub in
Windmill Hill.

Ingredients
6 sausages
2 red peppers
2 yellow peppers
1 tin of chopped tomatoes
1 bunch of flat-leaf parsley
A couple of sprigs of thyme
Pinch of salt and pepper

Following an ordeal, involving shorts, Cardiff
and rental vans I arrived home to find my
girlfriend had cooked this old family recipe.

Method
1. Chop sausages into bite-sized chunks and
   brown off in a pan with a little oil, and place
   in a casserole dish.
2. Repeat above process with the peppers.
3. Roughly chop the parsley and pick the leaves
   from the thyme and add to the dish.
4. Add the tin of tomatoes, salt and pepper and
   half a tin of water.
5. Cook in a pre-heated oven (180°C) for 45
   mins.
6. Serve with crusty bread and remember to
   smash all plates afterwards!

TOP TIP
Try using spicy sausages or other varieties of sausage to make the stew different.

Molletes

V

Origin
Mexican.

Recipe supplied by
Magali who lives with Steve on Hill Street. She grew up in Totterdown and moved back in 2007.

Ingredients
250 g black pinto beans
2 baguettes
2 small onions
Cheddar cheese, as much as you fancy
3 ripe tomatoes
Fresh coriander
1-2 small chilli peppers
Salt
Vegetable oil
Lime juice

Two years ago, we went on a trip of a lifetime, to visit our friends in Mexico. On our first night in their little house, we were feeling jet-lagged and ready for bed. Our friends had other ideas, however, and decided to throw a party in our honour. They came out of the kitchen with Mexican beers, tequila, limes, salt… and a tray of hot molletes. We were sold, and lived off the things for the rest of our month-long trip, eating them every single day. Now, whenever we're feeling fed up with the rain and cold in Bristol, we invite some friends round and cook up a tray of molletes.

Method
1. Put the black beans in a bowl, cover with 3 inches of water and leave to soak overnight.
2. Drain water, put beans in a saucepan, cover with 3 inches of water and cook for about 3 hours. Drain water, keeping about half a cupful back.
3. Put about a tablespoon of vegetable oil in a frying pan, add chopped onion, cook until translucent.
4. Add the beans and the water, and mash them all up, while they are cooking, with a potato masher. Add salt to taste.
5. To make the salsa, mix the chopped tomatoes, chopped coriander, chopped chilli pepper and some salt in a bowl. You can add a squeeze of lime juice if you like.
6. Heat the oven to about 200°C.
7. Slice the baguettes lengthwise. Spread the beans onto the bread, add some grated cheese and bake for about 10-15 mins.
8. Just before you serve, add some salsa on top.

TOP TIP

Cooking the beans is a bit of a faff, so you might as well cook up a big batch and freeze what you don't use for later. You can save it for Gallo pinto (rice and black beans) – another favourite! Or just buy the refried beans, or mash up a can of kidney beans with some fried onions.

---

awl (Vegetable Stew)

Origin
Wales.

Recipe supplied by
Richard Jones, Maggie, Caitlin and Mena Telfer who have lived in Balmain Street, Totterdown since 1999.

Ingredients
2 leeks, chopped
1 clove of garlic
6 carrots, roughly chopped
6 potatoes cut into chunks
Olive oil for frying
1 pint water/vegetable stock or stock cube
Salt and pepper
Pot pourri of fresh herbs from the garden (parsley, chives, rosemary, bay leaf, sage, mint, tansy, rosemary)

Serves four.

Cawl is the Welsh word for stew or broth, so there's no standard recipe. My Auntie Nanw lived on a hill farm in Snowdownia and used to boil her cawl in a pyrex bowl on top of the range. This is my adaptation of her recipe. We often have it as a quick family meal on Saturday lunchtime or teatime with fresh veg from our allotment at Perret's Park.

Method
1. Heat the oil in a saucepan. Add leeks, potatoes, carrots and garlic. Stir to prevent burning. Cook for about five mins and season.
2. Add water and fresh herbs.
3. Add a veg stock cube or bouillon.
4. Cook vigorously for 30 mins if you're in a hurry or at a lower heat for 45 – 60 mins. Keep adding water if it dries out to get the cawl to the consistency you like.
5. Season and serve with crusty bread.

PICTURE: *Caitlin Telfer with freshly picked leeks from the Perret's Park allotments.*

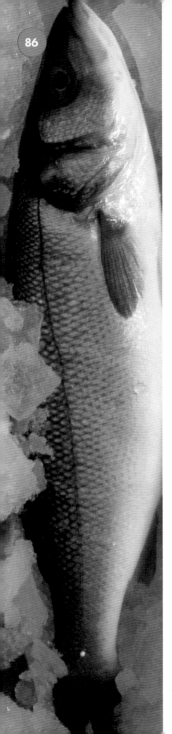

Hot Buttered Lobster

Origin
Totterdown.

Recipe supplied by
Darren at Charles Saunders Frozen Foods and Seafoods Specialists in Albert Road, St Philips. Charles Saunders has been trading in the area for more than 30 years and has a fish market where the public can buy fresh fish at wholesale prices, Tuesday to Friday from 7am to 4pm.

Ingredients
1 carrot
1 onion
1 litre water
150 ml white wine
Herbs
2 kg live lobster
170 g butter
1 lemon

Method
1. Slice the carrot and place in a saucepan with the water, wine and herbs. Bring to the boil, add the lobster and cover.
2. Steam until the lobster begins to change colour and speckle with red. Remove the pot from the heat and drain the lobster.
3. Open the lobster down the back and cut into two and remove the meat from the body and claws, together with all the green juices into a warm bowl wrapped in a tea towel.
4. Heat plenty of butter in a frying pan until foaming, add one helping at a time of the lobster meat and green juices and toss in the butter until cooked and the juices turn pink.
5. If necessary reheat the lobster shells in oven and spoon the meat back into the warm shells.
6. Finally put the remaining butter into a pan and scrape up any remaining bits. Pour into a hot sauce boat and pour over the lobsters.
7. Serve with fresh lemon and green salad.

Gefillte Fish Terrine

Origin
Poland.

Recipe supplied by
Minnie Russell-Harris
of London and
Totterdown.

Ingredients
900 g (2 lb) minced
white fish
1 large onion, peeled
2 eggs
2 tsp salt
Pinch of white pepper
2 tsp sugar
1 tbsp oil
2 tbsp cold water
56 g (2 oz) medium
matzo meal
28 g (1 oz) ground
almonds
2 large carrots, peeled
and finely grated

This is a firm family favourite and a delicious alternative to fishballs.

Method
1. Mix together puree onion, eggs, seasoning, oil and water. Then add the matzo meal and ground almonds, leaving the mixture for a few minutes.
2. Next add the minced fish, mix well and leave for five mins.
3. Heat the oven to 350°F (180°C). Choose a loaf-shaped container made of Pyrex, foil or tin 23cm x 13cm x 8cm (9in x 5in x 3in) and grease with cooking oil. Line the base with silicone paper.
4. Spoon half the fish into the container and press it down well; add the grated carrots, finishing with the remaining fish. Using the back of a spoon, press the contents of the container until firm.
5. Cover with a piece of greaseproof paper then cover completely with foil, tucking it round the outside.
6. Place the terrine in a bain marie with very hot water. Bake for 45-50 mins then remove from the oven and leave to cool, first having removed the foil and paper. When ready to turn out, run a knife round the edges and turn onto a dish. Serve with chrane* or pink mayonnaise if preferred.

*Chrane is a Jewish condiment. To make it, you'll need:
3 large cooked beetroots, vinegar, 2 sticks of horseradish and sugar. Peel and grate the beets and horseradish on a fine grater, then mix together. Pour over as much vinegar as the mixture will absorb and sweeten to taste.

Our Char's Boozy Stew

Origin
Totterdown.

Recipe supplied by
Charlotte Corcoran of Windsor Terrace and the Shakey who has lived in Totterdown since 2007, but it feels like years (in a good way).

Ingredients
Some booze (this can take the form of red wine, ale or Guinness)
Some casserole beef
Some bacon bits
Some veggies (mushrooms, carrots, peppers, broccoli – whatever you have in the fridge)
Some beef stock
A tin or two of chopped tomatoes
Loads of garlic and random herbs – I like to use loads of fresh thyme, but whatever dried herb mix you have on your spice rack is fine
Olive oil

Method
1. In a large pan, fry the garlic lightly in some olive oil, then add the bacon bits and beef, and brown.
2. While this is sizzling along, chop up the veggies, and chuck in the pan once the meat is browned. Fry for a bit until the veggies are also browning, then add your booze of choice and a good pint of stock.
3. Bring to the boil, add the tomatoes, and turn to a low heat. Put a lid on the pan, leave for ages and go and have a few glasses of wine with your friends (or do your housework/DIY as appropriate).
4. Leave to bubble away for at least 3 hours, checking and stirring every now and again. If the stew is getting dry, add more liquid – stock, booze and/or water. The longer this cooks, the better it will taste.
5. Serve with buttery baked or mashed potatoes, and more wine. Enjoy!

PICTURE: *Charlotte Corcoran in the kitchen of her home in Windsor Terrace.*

TOP TIP
If in doubt about how much booze to add, just add more booze!

Thai-style Vegetable (or salmon) Coconut Soup

Origin
Bristol. This is not authentic Thai!

Recipe supplied by
Suzanne Pearson of Hill Street who has lived in Totterdown since 1984.

Ingredients
Tin of coconut milk
Light cooking oil such as sunflower
1-2 vegetable stock cubes
Nam pla fish sauce (if adding salmon), follow instructions on bottle
Inch of ginger root, grated
Half a plump red chilli (avoid birds eye chillies) de-seeded and cut into rings
Large onion or spring onions, sliced into strips
2 large carrots, cut in half and cut into strips
1 red pepper de-seeded and cut into strips
Broccoli florets
2 courgettes cut in half then into strips
Handful of long green beans, cut off ends
2 Pak Choi or green cabbage, shredded
Medium thick noodles (straight to the wok range)
Salmon fillets for 4 (optional)

Serves four approx. You will need a large wok.

I started to cook this when our eldest daughter Viv came back from a trip round the world. She is vegetarian and raved about the food in Thailand so I made up a recipe! This recipe is more a stew than soup. We serve it in deep bowls and eat it as a main course. The recipe can be either vegetarian/vegan or a piece of salmon can be added. Select vegetables based on what is in season.

Method
1. Start by preparing all the ingredients.
2. Heat oil in the wok.
3. Stir fry onion strips for a minute until softening.
4. Add carrots and peppers and stir-fry, add grated ginger and red chilli.
5. Add beans and broccoli, stir-fry for a couple of minutes. Add courgettes and stir-fry.
6. Open coconut milk and pour over ingredients, rinse the tin out with water and add.
7. Add vegetable stock cubes (and fish sauce if adding salmon).
8. Boil kettle and add boiled water to cover the ingredients.
9. Simmer for 5 minutes or until vegetables are cooked to your liking
10. Add noodles and serve in deep bowls.

TOP TIP
If using salmon, place salmon fillets on the top of the simmering ingredients until they are cooked.

Cheese and Potato Pudding

Origin
British.

Recipe supplied by
Philip Harris of Pylle Hill Crescent, resident of Totterdown since 1980.

Ingredients
4 large potatoes
½ lb cheese (mainly cheddar but try adding those bits of other cheese left in the fridge)
One large onion
About ½ pint milk
2 eggs
1 oz butter
2 tbsp plain flour
Salt and pepper
Nutmeg (a must ingredient: too little is bland; too much is insane)
Breadcrumbs

Serves four.

I got this recipe from my first vegetarian cookbook and it was the first thing I baked. It is a celebration of potato, cheese and nutmeg and a reminder that cooking has no national boundaries.

Method
1. Peel and slice the potatoes thickly and boil for 10 mins.
2. Butter a large casserole dish.
3. Grate the cheese and chop the onion.
4. Layer the ingredients in the dish: potato, a little onion, cheese and repeat the layers until all ingredients are used up.
5. Beat the eggs with the flour with vigour or a whisk. Add the milk, salt and pepper, and the magic nutmeg (careful).
6. Pour the mix over the ingredients in the dish until it just reaches the top.
7. Cover the top in breadcrumbs.
8. Bake for about an hour at 180°C/gas mark 4 until well browned and puffed-out like a toad. Serve with vegetables and eat sitting on toadstools.

Fig and Goats' Cheese Tart

Origin
Mediterranean.

Recipe supplied by
Mark Fletcher of Fig.1,
St Luke's Road,
Totterdown.

Ingredients
For the pastry
340 g /12 oz plain
flour
120 g /4 oz butter
1 egg yolk
2 tbsp milk

For the filling
2 large eggs
240 g ricotta
240 g harder goats'
cheese such as chevre
or (preferably) a nice
Somerset goats' cheese
6 fresh figs

Our family businesses when we were growing up were restaurants. My mum is half Greek and half Maltese so much of her food is influenced by Mediterranean cuisine. Her mum and dad also ran cafes, shops and delicatessens so I guess it is no coincidence that I have eventually opened a shop myself here in Totterdown and, although it isn't a food shop, it does have food in the name.

This recipe is one we used to make in the restaurant and was always a firm favourite. Although it is obviously a Mediterranean recipe I like to substitute the cheeses with local cheeses where possible. I am also thrilled that Gerry at the Banana Boat, our local veg shop, is a big fan of figs as he often has them in. They are best eaten in season and I often eye up the huge fig trees growing next to the river near Temple Meads. If it wasn't for the car fumes they absorb day in, day out, I'd have scrambled up those trees by now to see how edible the fruit is!

Method
1. To make the pastry, ensure the butter is soft, cut into small cubes and place in a bowl with the flour. Crumb these together.
2. Whisk together the egg yolk and the milk. Make a well in the centre of the crumbs and pour in the milk and egg mix.
3. Mix the wet and dry ingredients together with your finger tips. If necessary adding a little extra milk until a dough is formed. Wrap this in cling film and place in the fridge for at least 1 hour. This makes it much easier to roll.
4. Whisk the eggs and ricotta together for the filling. Slice up goats' cheese and crumble into the egg mix, mixing thoroughly. Season the filling but

TOP TIP
For alternative seasonal toppings, replace figs with pear and toasted walnuts or with oven-roasted cherry tomatoes.

remember the goats' cheese can be salty so don't add too much. Pre-heat oven to 180°C. Grease a 25cm loose-bottomed flan tin.

5. Once the pastry is chilled, dust your work surface and a rolling pin with flour and then roll out pastry to an even round big enough for the tin. Line the tin with the pastry. In the restaurant we would always leave most of the spare pastry hanging over the edge of the tin to trim off after the tart is baked whilst it is still in the tin. This gives a professional neat finish and saves the pastry shrinking back below the top of the tin.

6. Spread the filling evenly over the pastry and then gently pour in the ricotta and egg mixture. Bake for 30 mins.

7. If the skins of the fig are tough then gently peel off the outer layer, but I think this is a rustic recipe so I don't often bother and just go straight ahead and quarter them. After 30 mins baking, take the tart out of the oven and arrange the figs over the top of the tart. Pop it back into the oven for a final 10 mins. Leave to cool before serving for the whole thing to firm up.

Paneer Kofta

Origin
Delhi.

Recipe supplied by
Panna Patel from
Patco, Wells Road,
Totterdown.

Ingredients
200 g paneer
2 tbsp plain flour or
corn flour
Oil for frying
Onion, chopped
Garlic, chopped
Green chilli, chopped
Tomatoes, tinned or
fresh
Double cream
Garam masala
2 tsp coriander powder
Turmeric
Salt
Coconut for garnishing
Fresh coriander
1 tsp sugar

*Cooking time: 15 – 20
mins.*

Method
1. Take paneer, add flour, chopped chilli and salt according to taste and mix to make a dough.
2. Make about 10-15 small balls from the dough and deep fry on medium heat.
3. Stir fry chopped onion until light brown and add chopped tomatoes, 1tbsp tomato puree, garlic, chilli, salt, turmeric.
4. Stir well and add ½ cup of water, 1tsp sugar, garam masala and mix.
5. Add double cream, mix well and add paneer fried balls and cook for 2 mins.
6. Garnish with coconut and fresh coriander and serve with nan, partha or chipatti and basmati rice.

PANNA'S TOP SPICE TIPS
1. For very spicy curry use milk to mild it down and stir well.
2. Use mustard seed. Put in hot oil first and let it pop.
3. Use garlic in cooking, chopped and fry it in oil until golden brown.
4. Use cumin seed. Fry in hot oil.
5. Cook with garam masala, add just before your dish is ready for good flavour.
6. Don't use too much onion in curry, it can upset your stomach.
7. If curry is very thin add some double cream.
8. Instead of curry powder add all the different spices to your curry to find a better taste.
9. Add fresh coriander just before serving food.
10. If you need any top tips for cooking curries, Panna from Patco will help you!

PICTURE: *Panna Patel with some of the ingredients for Paneer Kofta at Patco.*

est Indian chicken stew (curry)

Origin
West Indies.

Recipe supplied by
Vishnu who has lived in Totterdown since the 1970s.

Ingredients
1 cup of water
½ cup sunflower oil
8 chicken thighs, skinned
1 chopped onion
3 cloves garlic, crushed
2 tsp salt
1 tsp chilli powder
1 tbsp garam masala
2 tbsp of demerara sugar

Serves four.

When my mother came to the UK from Trinidad in 1962, she introduced this recipe to my family. It is now used frequently at many family occasions. Enjoy!

Method
1. Add the chopped onions to the heated sunflower oil and brown.
2. Add the chicken thighs and brown demerara sugar.
3. Once sugar is melted and the chicken is browning, add the remaining ingredients.
4. Add 1 cup of water and simmer for 30 mins.
5. Garnish with chopped coriander and fresh green chillies.

PICTURE: *Vishnu is well known for his Vish's Dishes food stall at the Art Trail and other community events.*

Thunderbolt Beef Sausage Casserole

. . . .

Origin
Bristol.

Recipe supplied by
The Thunderbolt, Bath Road, Totterdown.

Ingredients
6 organic local beef sausages (about 1lb)
1 lb beef chucks, cut into 1-inch pieces
1 large onion, sliced
2 medium cloves garlic, minced
2 medium green bell peppers, seeded and cut into eighths
4 medium potatoes, peeled and cut into quarters
2 cans kidney beans, drained
1 tsp basil
1 tsp salt
1 tsp pepper
2 beef bouillon cubes dissolved in boiling water

Method
1. In a heavy skillet over medium heat, brown sausages well and place in a casserole dish.
2. Drain fat from skillet, reserving 2 tbsp*. Brown beef in 1tbsp fat, then turn out into casserole.
3. Cook onion and garlic in remaining 1tbsp of fat until tender; add green peppers and cook one minute longer, stirring; turn out into casserole.
4. Add potatoes and beans to casserole.
5. Sprinkle with seasonings and mix lightly. Add bouillon. Cover and bake in a 350°F oven for 1 hour 15 mins or until beef and potatoes are tender.

For less saturated fat and less fat in general, dump all of the sausage fat and use a teaspoon or two of canola oil as necessary.

PICTURE: *Sophie MacDonald behind the bar at The Thunderbolt.*

TASTE OF TOTTERDOWN - MAINS

gni (Spaghetti in Hot Sauce)

Origin
Eritrea and Ethiopia.

Recipe supplied by
Sarah Burkin from Windmill Hill who
has lived in the area since 2000.

Ingredients
1 lb minced beef
2 medium onions, chopped
3 tbsp olive oil
2 tsp Berbere pepper or hot sauce
1 can chopped tomatoes
½ tsp salt
1 lb spaghetti, cooked
2 cups chicken broth (or chicken stock cubes)

For the Berbere (hot) sauce
1 tsp ground ginger
½ tsp ground coriander
½ tsp ground cardamon
½ tsp ground fenugreek
¼ tsp ground cloves
¼ tsp ground allspice
¼ tsp ground cinnamon
1 tbsp salt
5 tbsp cayenne pepper
2 tbsp paprika
1 tsp fresh ground black pepper

I suppose the best way to describe this is as an
Eritrean version of spaghetti bolognaise.

Method
1. To make the Berbere sauce combine the spices
   and roast in a dry skillet on a low to moderate
   heat stirring constantly for 5-10 mins or until
   roasted. Keep in a tight jar. Beware this is
   extremely hot, you may wish to add less
   cayenne.
2. Brown 1 lb of minced beef in pan with oil.
3. Add onion and sauté for 5 mins.
4. Add 2 tsp Berbere and simmer for 5 mins.
5. Add tomato paste, salt and two cups of stock.
6. Simmer for 20 mins.
7. Pour over spaghetti and serve.

Salmon, Broccoli Pasta

Origin
Totterdown.

Recipe supplied by
Hillcrest Primary School, School Road, Totterdown.

Ingredients
500 g tinned pink salmon
170 g macaroni
500 g broccoli spears
5 ml lemon juice
Mixed herbs to taste
Seasoning to taste
60 g plain flour
60 g milk powder
600 ml water
100 g grated cheese
Garlic puree to taste
15 g margarine

Makes 10 portions.

Method
1. Cook the pasta and broccoli separately until cooked but still firm, approx 15 mins.
2. Bone salmon and break into approx ½ inch pieces and place in the bottom of a greased tin.
3. To make up sauce, mix dried milk, flour, lemon juice, garlic puree, herbs and seasoning with water. Add the margarine and gently bring to the boil whisking all the time.
4. When the sauce has thickened, add half the grated cheese and reserve the rest.
5. Taste and adjust seasoning if necessary.
6. Add the pasta and the broccoli to the sauce then pour over the salmon, sprinkle with the rest of the grated cheese over the top.
7. Brown in oven or under grill.

TOP TIP
½ tsp mustard added at the beginning of the sauce will bring out the flavour of the cheese.

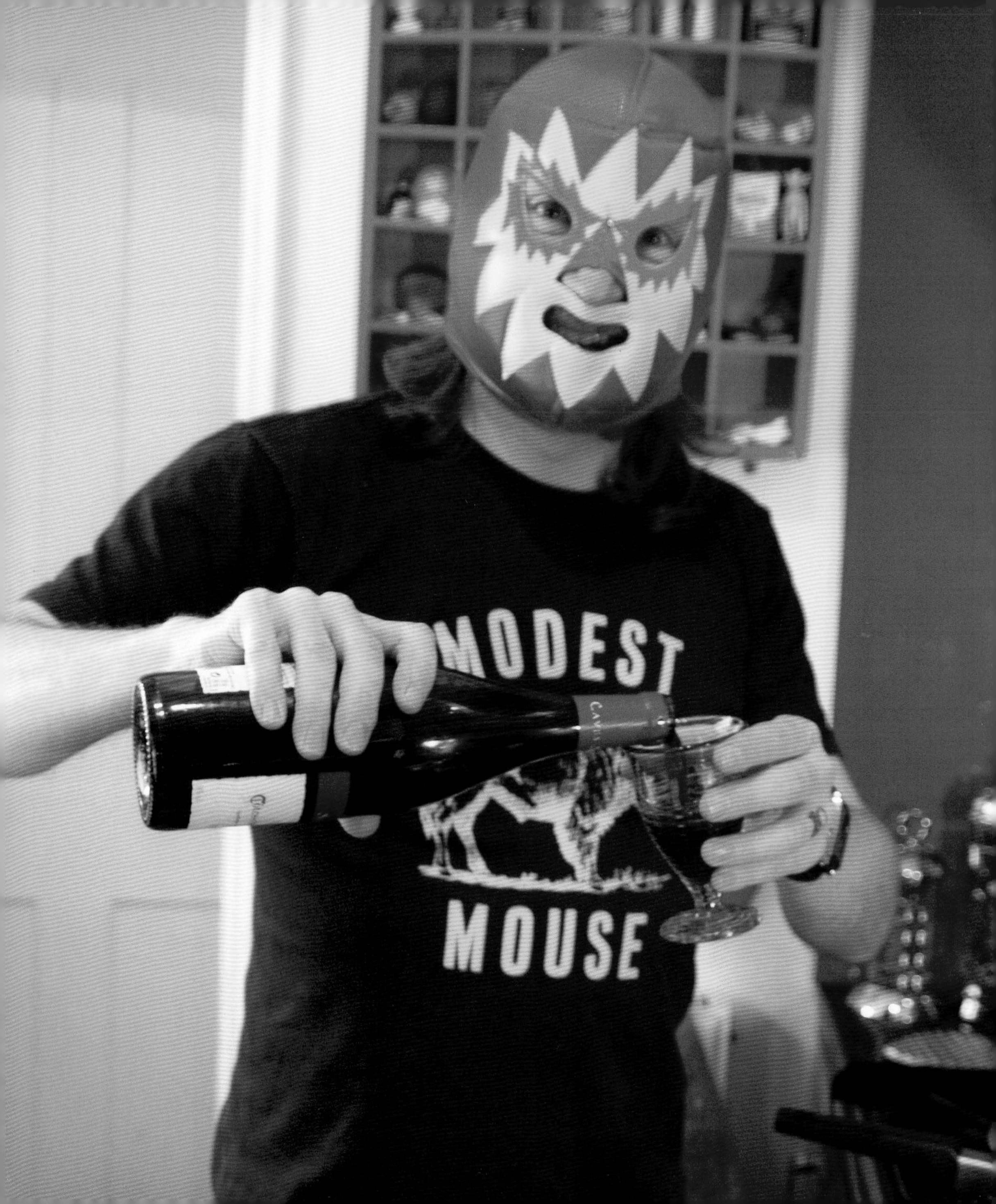
MODEST
MOUSE

Pasta La Vista, Maybe

Origin
Bristolian.

Recipe supplied by
The Law of Stevens Crescent, a Totterdown resident since 1998.

Ingredients
1 can chopped tomatoes
Tomato purée or concentrate
Small glass of red wine
Good slug of (veggie) Worcestershire sauce or mushroom ketchup
Fresh chopped basil (or dried if none available)
Couple of bay leaves
Vegetable stock cube
Salt and pepper to taste

Serves two.

Empty the tomatoes out of the can
And into the cleanest available pan.

Half-fill the can with the finest tap water
Pour into the pan and have a quick snorter

Of wine for yourself, then add a full glass.
The sauce goes in next (although you could pass

If there's none in the house). Add salt, pepper and herb
Then mix them all up for a pasta superb!

Have some wine yet again and then contemplate
How much to squeeze from the tom' concentrate

Turn on the heat for about half an hour
Simmer and stir but before you devour

The sauce should have shrunk to about half its size
And be lovely and gloopy from what you surmise.

Finally, here is a simple cook's trick
Add a veggie stock cube if you like it real thick.

The rest's up to you – this serves as a base
For all kinds of concoctions and dishes to taste.

PICTURE: *The masked poet chef of Totterdown.*

TOP TIP
Keep the opened bottle of wine with you in the kitchen and taste regularly to make sure it hasn't gone off.

arszcz (Beetroot Stew)

Origin
Central and Eastern Europe.

Recipe supplied by
Marie-Helene Kutek, Beaulieu, France (formerly of Upper Street, Totterdown).

Ingredients
Vegetables to make a stock: onion, shallot, carrot, parsnip and/or leek
A generous pinch of dried mushrooms
2 or 3 beetroot, depending on size
Salt, pepper and lemon juice for seasoning
Dill, chives or flat leaved parsley to garnish
Oil for sweating veg to make stock
Stock cube (optional)
Water

Barszcz or borscht, as you might know it, is claimed as belonging to many regions in central and eastern Europe. Another claim has been lain in Totterdown. The Totterdown version is a creation that is more than an amalgam of what has gone before, providing rich variations to suit most palates. It can be eaten as a clear soup, a stew or even a creamed soup, whizzed through a processor. Some serve it piping hot, whilst others prefer it chilled. I am sure that you will find your own favourite. The ingredient common to all versions is the beetroot.

Method
1. Traditionally, a wholesome beef stock was used as a base for the dish. In Totterdown, we make a vegetable stock, using seasonal produce or what is found in the veg store – one or two onions, a carrot plus anything you might fancy. Finely chop the veg and sweat in a large pan, with a little oil. It is best to stir frequently so that sticking to the bottom of the pan is kept to a minimum.
2. While this is sweating, and you are not stirring with your wooden spoon, peel and finely cube the washed beetroot. When the veg in the pan

---

TOP TIP
To add extra richness and depth to dishes, put a few dried mushrooms into a small container and cover with boiling water. Steep overnight.

starts to fill your kitchen with mouth-watering aromas, add the cubed beetroot, stir it through so that its colour touches all the other ingredients.

3. After a couple of minutes on a modest heat (never allow the pan to come to the boil), add the mushrooms with their juice and stir. After a couple of minutes, add sufficient water to cover the contents and a little over, a little being about 1in or 2.5cm.

4. Simmer until there is a deep colour, remembering not to boil the contents. I find that it takes about 10-15 mins. Taste and season.

5. This is sometimes when a stock cube comes in handy. If the veg are very fresh, the stock cube is not needed. Adding a stock cube means another couple of minutes on the hob.

6. Then, a squeeze of lemon, a twist of pepper and a sprinkle of salt and you should be ready to serve.

7. A garnish of freshly chopped herbs makes a great contrast to the deep colour of the dish. A dollop of cream creates the most dazzling colour. You'll just have to try it.

Traditional variations include: clear soup, served on its own or with little savoury pastries, with or without cream and clear soup with a boiled egg garnish. Some years ago, a Vale Street neighbour made the basic soup, adding potatoes, which just melted during cooking, making a thoroughly delicious and warming winter soup. A favourite of mine is eating the soup chilled, with cream, and loads of chopped herbs. Bon appetit!

ambar

Origin
South India.

Recipe supplied by
The Extraordinary Travelling Thali Cafe,
William Street, Totterdown.

Ingredients
Sambar mix
A good pinch of...
Coriander
Chillies
Cumin
Fenugreek
Mustard seeds
Turmeric
Black gram dhal
Asafoetida

Ingredients
Dhal
100 g toor dhal
20 g tamarind
4 drumsticks (South Indian long vegetable, guess what it looks like)
1 large onion, diced
1 doodhi (Indian marrow), peeled and cubed
4-5 curry leaves

Serves four.

This simple yet delicious dish is eaten daily by millions in Southern India and it always goes down well in our restaurants. Its fresh and distinctive taste has all the comfort of dhal with an extra something that makes it really special. We first cooked Sambar for our staff working the night shift at Bestival; Sid's mum took one look at the hungry faces and gave us the recipe – it was an instant hit! In 2008 we opened our Thali Café in the old Glasnost building. What a great area, loving the views.

Method
1. Grind together the ingredients for the Sambar mix with a pestle and mortar.
2. Boil toor dhal in 1 pint of water with drumsticks for half hour.
3. Add sambar mix and slowly cook.
4. Add dhoodi and cook until soft.
5. Add tamarind and season to taste.
6. Heat 2 tbsp of oil in a frying pan and add the diced onion, red chilli and curry leaves.
7. Add a pinch of hing (asafoetida). Fry until onions are translucent. Add to Sambar sauce.
8. Boil for further 5 mins.
9. Serve hot and enjoy!

Spinach-stuffed Cannelloni

Origin
Italy.

Recipe supplied by
Barry Horton of Hill Street, a Totterdown local since 1991.

Ingredients
10-12 cannelloni tubes
2-3 slices cooked ham, cut into small bits
Bag of frozen spinach (they are in small balls in a frozen packet). It is best to thaw the spinach out before you start the recipe. I find you usually need 12 to fill 10 cannelloni tubes.
8 medium mushrooms, sliced
Big tin tomatoes with herbs
Enough cheese to grate over top of dish

Serves two big portions.

This came from a website and I doctored to suit. If I can make it taste good then so can anyone!

Method
1. Drain some of the excess moisture out of the spinach.
2. Mix spinach and ham chunks (use fingers) and stuff this mix into the cannelloni tubes.
3. Place the filled tubes into the dish side by side.
4. Slice the mushrooms so they cover the tubes.
5. Mash up the tinned tomatoes, add a little water so it pours, and pour it over the cannelloni tubes and mushrooms.
6. Sprinkle the grated cheese over the top.
7. Put into pre-heated oven at 200°C/400°F or gas mark 6 for 40 minutes.

TOP TIP
Add chopped spring onion for extra flavour.

Hussami Kebabs

Origin
Middle East.

Recipe supplied by
Deb Gubbay from Balmain Street who
has lived in Totterdown since 1999.

Ingredients
2 chicken breasts
1 potato
1 red pepper
1 onion
Fresh ginger, grated
Garlic, chopped
Turmeric
Salt and pepper

This recipe comes from my great grandmother
who is Arabic.

Method
1. Mix up potato, red pepper and chicken cut
   into squares and thread onto kebab sticks.
2. In a casserole dish, fry an onion with a pinch
   of fresh ginger, fresh garlic, turmeric, salt and
   pepper in oil.
3. Add kebabs and turn to coat. Turn heat to low,
   cover casserole and cook until done.
4. The kebabs can be cooked in advance and
   then warmed up under a grill before serving.

Posh Poached Duck Eggs with Parsley, Tomato and Butter Sauce

Origin
Totterdown.

Recipe supplied by
Steve Russell and Jo Burr of Brecknock Road. Steve has lived in the area since 1999 and Jo since 1981.

Ingredients (per person)
2 duck eggs (chicken eggs can be used but they're not as posh)
1 English muffin
1 large tomato
1 glove of garlic
1 handful of fresh coarsely chopped parsley
40 g butter (approx)
1 cup malt vinegar
Salt and pepper

We first made this for breakfast with what we had lying around whilst living in Windsor Terrace. We've always liked proper poached eggs and therefore decided to adapt the egg and English muffin idea to something that was our own. Since the first time we made this, we haven't changed the recipe at all as it just worked. Almost all the ingredients are available from local Totterdown suppliers. We will show you how to cook delicious poached eggs in boiling water (the best way!), which a lot of people find hard. It's currently our favourite breakfast!

Method
1. Mostly fill a large pan with water and bring to the boil.
2. While the water is heating, cut the tomato into thick slices, finely chop the garlic and place in a saucepan with the butter and most of the parsley. You are only looking to really heat the tomato so cook at a very low heat. Let the garlic and parsley infuse into the butter. Avoid stirring at all and turn off the heat if they look like they're starting to mush.
3. Pour the vinegar into the boiling water and add a pinch of salt. Turn off the heat completely and wait for ALL the bubbles to disappear.
4. Crack the eggs in to the water and put a lid on. There should be no need to put the pan back on the heat. A large pan should provide space for around four eggs at a time. Put in the eggs as quickly as you can but more importantly, remember which order you put the eggs in because you should take them out in the order you put them in to ensure an equal cooking time. They should take about 4½ mins but the best way to tell when they are done is to prod the first inserted egg's white, around the

TOP TIP
Save some raw parsley to chew on after the meal to help get rid of the garlic smell which may otherwise remain with you for the rest of the day. Duck eggs are usually available from our friendly local greengrocers The Banana Boat. They also sell generous bunches of parsley.

yolk. When it is reasonably firm but the yolk is still quite soft they should be cooked.

5. As soon as you have put a lid on the eggs, cut the muffins in half and toast slowly on both sides until brown and crispy. Just before the eggs are ready, put the unbuttered muffins on a warm plate and pour most of the tomato, garlic and parsley sauce on and around them.

6. Use a ladle or similar to extract the eggs and place one on each muffin. Cover with the remaining sauce and parsley then season with ground pepper. Delicious!

A Nice Bit of Pork

Origin
Bristol.

Recipe supplied by
Isabel Sheppard of
The New Found Out
pub, Green Street,
Totterdown.

Ingredients
4 pork steaks (you will
need to flatten them out
to cook evenly)
1 lb Potatoes
Sage and onion stuffing
1 or 2 apples (can be
any kind)
Bisto gravy granules
An ovenproof dish
(ideally like a lasagne
dish)

I like one-pot cooking because it means less washing up! This is good comfort food on a cold winter's night!

Method
1. Peel and slice your potatoes fairly thin to ensure that they cook through.
2. Grease the dish and layer the potatoes on the bottom.
3. Mix up some gravy granules with some hot water. Make it as thick as you like it to be. Pour gravy over the potatoes and cover them.
4. Slice the apples up quite thin and put a layer on top of the potatoes and cover again with the gravy.
5. You will need to make sure your pork steaks are almost 1cm thin. To do this, place the pork steaks on top of a piece of cling film and place another over the top, then hammer thin with a rolling pin.
6. Put the pork on top of the apples and put another layer of gravy over the pork. Don't worry if you think you have too much gravy, while it is cooking, the gravy will get absorbed.
7. Making sure you have enough room at the top for your stuffing mix, put the dish in the oven on about 220°C for about 30 to 40 mins.
8. While this is in the oven, make up your stuffing mix.
9. After 40 mins, take the dish out of the oven, and pour some more gravy over the top of the meat so that it doesn't dry out and then put the stuffing mix on the top and cook as per the stuffing instructions. You may need a bit more gravy to serve with depending on your personal taste.

PICTURE: *There's a warm welcome and maybe a nice bit of pork at the New Found Out.*

CHEESE
FLAVOURED
MOMENTS
SAVOURY SELECTION
24x28g Packs
UMBRO
UMBRO
UMBRO
UMBRO
PEPSI
ER
COURAGE
BEST

DESSERTS JAM & DRINKS

chinese chews

Origin
Dublin.

Recipe supplied by
Jo Fox-Mills of Windsor Terrace who has lived in Totterdown since 2006.

Ingredients
100 g butter
100 g golden granulated sugar
2 eggs
100 g self-raising flour
200 g stoneless dates
50 g glacé cherries

Optional
25 g raisins
50 g pecan nuts
25 g walnuts

My paternal grandmother (from Dublin not China!) passed this recipe on to my mum and I have very fond memories of eating both my granny's and my mum's creations. History doesn't relate where the name came from! It is a constant source of debate in our family whether or not to put nuts in them. I am in the 'NO' camp.

Method
1. Cream the butter and sugar.
2. Add eggs and mix.
3. Fold in the flour.
4. Fold in the fruit (and nuts, if you must).
5. Put in a square/swiss roll tin.
6. Bake in a medium oven for 25 mins, or until brown.

TOP TIP
Don't put the nuts in!

Gran Shearer's Apple Cake

Origin
Scotland.

Recipe supplied by
Tina Shearer of Richmond Street, Totterdown.

Ingredients
2 lb cooking apples plus sugar to taste
8 oz self-raising flour
4 oz margerine or butter
4 oz sugar
2 eggs, beaten

This recipe was passed down from my grandmother, a great Scottish cook who, from what I can remember, loved to make and eat biscuits and cakes.

Method
1. Stew the apples with the sugar and strain off the juice.
2. Melt the margarine or butter and remove from heat.
3. Add the 4oz of sugar, beaten eggs and flour to the butter or margarine and mix together.
4. Line an 8-inch baking tray with baking parchment. Press in the dough and put apples on top.
5. Bake at gas mark 4 for about 50-60 mins.
6. Remove from oven and allow to cool slightly.
7. Serve warm with whipped double cream or eat cold on its own. Delicious!

Sticky Toffee Banana Bread

Origin
Bristol.

Recipe supplied by
Sarah Rogers of Arnos Street, Totterdown.

Ingredients
3 ripe bananas
2 eggs, beaten
4 oz butter
4 oz yoghurt (preferably toffee)
4 oz light brown sugar
8 oz self-raising flour (add ½ tsp baking powder)
5 oz walnuts, chopped
7 oz toffees, roughly chopped

Method
1. Heat oven to 160°C. Melt butter in a pan. Mix melted butter, yoghurt, beaten eggs, sugar and mashed bananas until combined. Line and butter a 900gm (2lb) loaf tin.
2. Sift flour into mixture, and fold until combined.
3. Fold in ¾ of chopped toffee and walnuts.
4. Pour mixture into lined loaf tin and sprinkle on top the remaining toffee and walnuts.
5. Bake for around 50 minutes until loaf has risen and feels springy.
6. Leave loaf in tin to cool.
7. Keep in airtight container, will last around 4 days.

Malteser and Baileys cheesecake

Made famous at Glasnost restaurant… definitely an indulgent dessert! Goes lovely with a glass of Baileys on ice and a pack of Maltesers. Pure yum!

Origin
British/Irish.

Recipe supplied by
Viv Maginnis of Hill Street who has lived in Totterdown since 1986.

Ingredients
1 large pack of gingernut biscuits
1 box of Maltesers
1 small cup of Baileys
1 tbsp cocoa powder
1 small cup caster sugar
2 tubs cream cheese (full fat please)
2 real vanilla pods
1 small cup double cream (if too stiff)
Third of a block of butter

You will need a large cake tin, about 2 or 2½ inches tall with removable base.

Method
1. Cover your cake tin with clingfilm so it fits around it entirely with plenty extra hanging out (to cover top at the end).
2. Melt butter in microwave, crush gingernut biscuits (I put them in a plastic bag, then wrapped in a tea towel and beat with a rolling pin, but you can whack them in the blender).
3. Mix crushed gingernuts and butter so all the gingernuts are evenly covered. Pour mixture into tin and pat down firmly and evenly all over.
4. Get a mixing bowl and add the cream cheese, caster sugar, cocoa powder and Baileys and mix together. It should be a fairly firm mixture, not too sloppy. If it's too stiff, add a little double cream.
5. Rub vanilla pods in between your fingers then slice open and scrape out vanilla seeds and add to cream cheese mixture.
6. Crush ¾ of the box of Maltesers (as you did the gingernuts)… not too fine, leave some nice big bits. Yum! Add to cream cheese mix and fold in.
7. Spoon mixture on top of gingernut base and pat down gently. Cover with rest of clingfilm and smooth top down.
8. Put in fridge for minimum of an hour. Take out and remove base, then remove clingfilm.
9. Decorate with left over Maltesers and eat it all before your friends come over!

TOP TIP
Taste the mixture before adding to the cake tin… if you think it needs more sugar or Baileys or Maltesers, add more!

Kulfi Ice cream

Origin
India.

Recipe supplied by
Debbie Gubbay from Balmain Street who has lived in Totterdown since 1999.

Ingredients
2 large tins evaporated milk
1 cup sugar
2 oz chopped pistachio nuts (not salted) or ground almonds
Saffron soaked in 1 tbsp warm milk

Serves eight.

Method
Blend all ingredients except nuts and freeze till soft. Stir, add half the nuts, refreeze until solid. Sprinkle with more pistachio nuts before serving.

Chocolate Truffle with Disaronno Amaretto and Almonds

Origin
European.

Recipe supplied by
Janey, the chef at Bocabar, Bath Road, Totterdown.

Ingredients
1 pint double cream
22 oz the very best dark chocolate (at least 75% cocoa solids)
1½ oz unsalted butter
2 generous shots Disaronno Amaretto (Italian almond liquer)
Handful of flaked almonds

We wanted something really luxurious and indulgent for the Bocabar deli-counter and this seems to do the trick! It is really rich and fixes the chocolate cravings a treat!

Method
1. Butter and line a 2-litre loaf tin with greaseproof paper, making sure the greaseproof is overhanging the tin. Stand on a flat baking sheet, this will make it easier to move to the fridge without any spills.
2. Gently warm the cream and chocolate together, stirring constantly until chocolate is completely melted. Do not let it boil or stick to bottom of pan. Take off heat, stir in butter until melted. Pour in the Amaretto, mix together. Allow to cool slightly, but not set.
3. Pour mixture into lined loaf tin, sprinkle the flaked almonds over the chocolate mixture allowing them to rest on top.
4. Carefully place in the fridge and let set over night.
5. To serve. When set, gently ease out the whole truffle 'loaf' and place on a flat surface.
6. Cut into slices and serve with seasonal fruit and more cream.

TOP TIP
Try different flavours and fillings – crushed digestive biscuits can be added, or Baileys instead of Amaretto, poached fruit and different nuts.

Pav

Origin
New Zealand and
Australia.

Recipe supplied by
Kate Pollard who lived
in Hill Street for 17
years and now lives in
King Street, Sydney.

Ingredients
6 egg whites
1½ cups caster sugar
Pinch cream of tartar
(increases volume and
crisps outside)
300 ml thickened cream
1 tbsp icing sugar
1 tsp vanilla essence
250 g strawberries,
hulled
2 kiwi fruit, peeled and
sliced
150 g blueberries (or
whatever decorative
fruit are available in the
UK)

*Serves eight – to be
made by at least three
people.*

New Zealand and Australia fight over national ownership of this dish (well NZ fights, Oz doesn't give a monkey's). No-one down under knows where PAV actually came from. My guess is Up-over originally. It's served at massive family gatherings at Christmas in NZ and is usually made as a group effort. My first intro to it was at my first Xmas in Auckland when my son's Maori in-laws gathered. Dinner was roasted chook and roast potatoes, pumpkin, squash and kumera (sweet potato), and loads of brown onion gravy. This is all roasted together in the oven, in the style of the Maori hangi, where it's roasted in a hole in the ground.

Method
Person 1
1. Pre-heat oven to 120°C or100°C fan-assisted.
2. Line a baking tray with baking paper.
3. Mark a 23 cm circle on the above.
4. Beat egg whites until stiff peaks form and then add caster sugar.
5. Beat for 10 mins or until sugar has dissolved. Add cream of tartar. Beat for 1 min. Spoon mixture onto circle. Using a palette knife or spatula shape into a circle with high sides. Make furrows up the sides.
6. Bake for an hour until firm. Turn off oven. Allow to cool in oven with door slightly ajar.

Person 2 (who has arrived with cream)
7. Beat cream, icing sugar and vanilla until peaks form. Place Pav on a serving plate. Top with cream mixture.

Person 3 (arriving with fruit)
8. Arranges the fruit in an artistic and over-the-top way on the Pav face.

Peaches Ice cream

Origin
Totterdown.

Recipe supplied by
Eamon Fullalove from the Star and Dove, St Luke's Road, Totterdown.

Ingredients
½ pint good orange juice
One cup of soft brown sugar
Fresh peaches

As your friends are wallowing in the glory of the burgers (see page 72 Mains section) you have served up, and the bar-b-q is cooling down, it's time to hit them with another winner...

Method

1. Put a heavy frying pan on the barbie and pour in the orange juice and soft brown sugar.
2. As this starts to boil, add some fresh peaches that you have cut in half and removed the stone – allow one for each person. Be sure to put them in cut-face down.
3. Let them simmer for 5 minutes and then flip them over with a fork (mind the caramel juice, it's hotter than hell.)
4. Place a small knob of butter into each peach (about 1tsp worth). When the butter melts, they are ready.
5. Put the peaches in a bowl cut-side up and place a ball of good vanilla ice cream in each peach and pour over the caramel that is left in the pan.
6. If you really want to get the prize, you can sprinkle the whole thing with crushed amaretti biscuits or macaroons – sorted!

TOP TIP
If you really can't get hold of any fresh peaches you can use tinned... just make the caramel with half the orange juice and half the syrup from the peaches and don't add the brown sugar but don't say we didn't warn you!

Tiramisù (meaning 'pick me up' in Italian)

Origin
Sicily.

Recipe supplied by
Giovanna Pace of the Banana Boat, Oxford Street. The Banana Boat has been in Totterdown since about 1988. We have been here since 1996.

Ingredients
500 g mascarpone
2 eggs
200 g sugar (or to your liking)
1 tbsp vanilla essence
Espresso coffee
Savoiardi biscuits (trifle sponge fingers)
Kahlúa liqueur (or any other liqueur – Baileys is good)
Drinking chocolate powder
Cream

Method
1. Mix egg white until a soft meringue.
2. Mix mascarpone, sugar, vanilla and egg yolk all together, adding a bit of cream or Kahlúa if needed to thin mixture.
3. Fold in egg white.
4. Make espresso coffee and put in a bowl to cool a little. Add sugar and Kahlúa to your acquired taste.
5. Dip your trifle biscuits in the coffee one at a time and layer in a dish. Layer the mascarpone over the biscuits and dust with chocolate powder.
6. Repeat again with as many layers as you want (three is best).
7. Top off the Tiramisù with mascarpone cheese and dust with chocolate powder.
8. This can be eaten straight away or popped in the fridge for later (if you can wait that long!)

TOP TIP
Please note, if pregnant, this can be made without egg. Just add a bit more cream to thin the mixture out. For children – leave out alcohol and in between each layer of biscuit and cream, add a layer of chocolate chips (white choc chips are best).

ardamom cake

Recipe supplied by
Sarah Jasna Heubach
from Organique,
Wells Road,
Totterdown.

Ingredients
For the cake:
1 tsp whole green
cardamom pods
175 g butter
100 g light brown
sugar
3 medium eggs
225 g plain flour
1½ tsp baking powder
½ tsp bicarbonate of
soda
50 g ground almonds
142 ml cream
Finely grated rind and
juice of 2 lemons

For the topping:
25 g butter
50 g plain flour
25 g caster sugar
100 g pack flaked
almonds
Icing sugar

A classic cake recipe.

Method
1. Pre-heat oven to 180°C or gas mark 4. Grease and line a 20 cm tin.
2. Using a pestle and mortar, crush the cardamom pods to split them open.
3. Separate the black seed inside and discard the green husks.
4. Crush the black seeds finely.
5. Beat together the butter and sugar until light and fluffy. Add the eggs, beating well.
6. Sift the flour, baking powder and bicarbonate of soda and fold into the mixture.
7. Fold the crushed cardamom into the mixture, then the almonds, cream and lemon rind and juice.
8. Spoon the mixture into the tin.
9. Make the topping by rubbing the butter into the flour until it resembles fine breadcrumbs. Stir in the sugar and almonds. Sprinkle over the cake mixture.
10. Bake until well risen and firm – approx 50 mins then allow to cool before removing from the tin. Dust with icing sugar.

Welsh Cakes

Origin
Welsh.

Recipe supplied by
John Evans of Windsor Terrace who has lived in Totterdown since 2006.

Ingredients
1 egg
8 oz self-raising flour
4 oz Welsh butter or lard
3 oz currants
3 oz caster sugar
Milk if required

The recipe for Welsh cakes has been used by our family for generations. I have fond memories of eating my mother's and grandmother's Welsh cakes with a cup of tea during my childhood, and being a very popular man in university when I took some back for my friends to sample.

Method
1. Sieve the flour. Rub the butter in the flour.
2. Mix all the ingredients together in a bowl to make a pastry ball. Add milk as required.
3. Roll out with a rolling pin to approx 1 inch thick. Cut out circles of 2 inch to 3 inch.
4. Moderately heat the hot plate, griddle or baking stone (we use a chapatti pan) and drop on the Welsh cakes. Cook until brown and flip over.
5. When cooked, sprinkle with sugar and eat warm or leave to cool and reheat before eating.

TOP TIP
An alternative to currants is to use finely chopped apple to make Shenkin.

Mungu's Chocolate Cake

Origin
Wales.

Recipe supplied by
Mia Harris from Pylle Hill Crescent who has lived in Totterdown on and off, all her life.

Ingredients
Cake
6 oz caster sugar
6 oz butter/margarine
6 oz self-raising flour
2 large eggs
1 dessert spoon cocoa powder
1 tsp coffee granules

Filling
2 oz butter
4 oz icing sugar
1 dessert spoon cocoa
1 tbsp coffee granules

Topping
1 medium bar of milk chocolate

This is my Mungu's recipe (Welsh grandma). She has been making this cake since my brother and I were little and always packs us off with some cake whenever we visit her in Wales. Since we have grown up a bit she has kindly baked more and we each get a cake in a Cadbury's Roses tin to take home with us. It's a lovely cake and goes well with a nice cup of tea.

Method
Instructions for cake
1. Cream butter and caster sugar.
2. Mix a little bit of hot water (not boiling) in a jug with cocoa powder and coffee (not too thick or runny) and mix in with butter and sugar.
3. Beat eggs and add to mixture.
4. Add sifted flour.
5. Grease tin with butter. Shake 1 teaspoon of flour around tin until evenly coated and empty out excess flour. This prevents the cake from sticking.
6. Divide mixture into 2 circular sponge tins approx 1.5 inches deep and 7.5 inches wide.
7. Place in the oven on gas mark 4 until brown for approx 20-25 mins.
8. The sides will shrink when the cake is ready.
9. Put onto a wire rack when ready.

Filling
1. Beat the butter and sugar until creamy.
2. Mix 1 dessert spoon of cocoa and coffee in a cup of hot (not boiling) water, add together with mixture and beat.
3. Spread between the two layers.

Toppings
1. Heat chocolate over hot water in a basin until it dissolves.
2. Spread over the cake top quickly before it hardens.

Sticky Chocolate Biscuit Cake

Origin
Bristol.

Recipe supplied by
Windmill Hill City Farm.

Ingredients
125 g unsalted butter
200 g Maya Gold chocolate (or plain good
quality dark chocolate)
75 g golden syrup
100 g digestive biscuits
50 g sultanas

Makes around 10 small, thin slices.

This is the most famous cake cooked in our café,
and the slices fly from our hands.

Method
1. Line a small loaf tin with clingfilm or baking
   parchment.
2. Melt the butter and syrup in a small pan and
   heat until just boiling.
3. Melt the chocolate over a pan of simmering
   water (or in the microwave).
4. Mix the chocolate and buttery syrup together.
5. Crush the biscuits but not too small because
   they break up further whilst mixing.
6. Add biscuits and sultanas to the mixture. Mix.
7. Pour mixture into the lined container, smooth
   over the top and when cool, place in the fridge
   for at least 4 hours to set.

TOP TIP
Do add walnuts and glacé cherries if you like; the cherries look good as decoration on the top. This
is VERY rich indeed. Small slices only are needed and it is a very adult version of this childhood
classic. This needs to be kept in the fridge to keep a firm texture.

Pot of Vanilla and Cinnamon Hot Cocoa

Origin
Bristol.

Recipe supplied by
Sarah Jasna Heubach from Organique,
Wells Road, Totterdown.

Ingredients
6 cups of milk
5 tsp cocoa powder
½ cup maple syrup
½ tsp ground cinnamon
1 tsp vanilla extract
½ cup double cream whipped
Pinch of grated nutmeg

It's worth taking a little extra time to make this fantastic version of hot cocoa.

Method
1. Whisk the cocoa powder and 8 tbsp of milk to a smooth paste, then add the maple syrup and ground cinnamon continuing to whisk.
2. Add the mixture to the remaining milk in a pot over low heat.
3. Simmer for 10 mins. Remove from the heat and stir in the vanilla extract.
4. Serve topped with whipped cream and a hint of grated nutmeg.

Gwendolyn's Famous Chocolate Chip Cookies

Origin
Canada.

Recipe supplied by
Jack and Jill Toy Shop and Dulseigh Pomerance-Trifts on Wells Road. The shop was established in 2001. We took over as the new management in 2007.

Ingredients
1 cup/200 g shortening/butter/margarine
100 g white sugar
100 g brown sugar
2 eggs
1 tsp vanilla extract
1 tsp salt
1 tsp bicarbonate of soda
1½ cups/200 g plain flour
1½ cups/200 g chocolate chips
2 cups/250 g rolled oats

This recipe was given to me in 1991 by a good childhood friend who made me a huge box of cookies to keep me happy on a flight home from Vancouver. They have kept me happy in many moments of stress over the years. Despite the high sugar content, the oats are a wonderful source of slow-release energy (and promote milk production for breast feeding mums) and the chocolate is high in iron! Oh, and boy do they taste great!

Method
1. Cream the butter.
2. Add sugars gradually.
3. Add eggs and beat well.
4. Add vanilla extract.
5. Sift together flour, salt and soda.
6. Add to creamed mixture.
7. Add nuts, chocolate and oatmeal.
8. Drop by the teaspoonful onto a greased cookie sheet.
9. Bake at 350°F/180°C for 10 – 12 mins.

TOP TIP
You can omit the chocolate and/or nuts and add some sultanas or chopped dried apricots for a healthier version – still tastes great! Try adding a teaspoon of cinnamon and/or ginger for a winter festive season taste!

Lounger's chocolate Brownie

• •

Origin
Bristolian.

Recipe supplied by
Recipe supplied by Benedict John Harding from the Banco Lounge, Wells Road, Totterdown which opened in 2006.

Ingredients
170 g butter
215 g dark chocolate
4 free-range eggs
170 g self-raising flour
450 g caster sugar
100 g hazelnuts (optional)

The chocolate brownie has been on Lounge's menu in some form since the original Lounge opened in Bedminster in August 2002. The present version came in June 2003 when I joined the company to open Tinto Lounge and remains a firm favourite with our customers to this day. It has been voted one of the 20 best things to eat in Bristol by Venue magazine.

Method
1. Melt the butter and chocolate together.
2. Whisk in the eggs.
3. Fold in flour, sugar and nuts if using.
4. Place in a tray lined with baking parchment and bake at 180°C for approximately 30 minutes, until set on top but still slightly soft in the centre.
5. Serve with vanilla ice cream and chocolate sauce.

PICTURE: *Staff at the Banco Lounge on Wells Road.*

Rhubarb and Ginger Jam

Origin
Hertfordshire.

Recipe supplied by
Kim Woods who lives
in Upper Street,
Totterdown.

Ingredients
Makes 1.4 kg
1.1 kg rhubarb,
chopped
1.1 kg sugar
Juice of 2 lemons
25 g fresh root ginger
110 g preserved or
chopped crystallised
ginger

My grandparents used to live in Kneesworth, Hertfordshire and visiting them from London used to feel like a big trip to the countryside when I was a child. They had plum and apple trees in the garden and a wealth of blackberries growing in the hedgerows in the surrounding lanes. My Nan used to make lots of lovely jam, here's one of her favourites.

Method
1. Put the rhubarb in a large bowl in alternate layers with the sugar and lemon juice. Cover and leave overnight.
2. Next day, bruise the ginger root slightly with a weight or rolling pin then wrap in a piece of muslin. Put the rhubarb mixture into a preserving pan with the muslin bag and bring to the boil. Boil rapidly for 15 minutes.
3. Remove the muslin bag, add the preserved or crystallised ginger and boil for a further 5 minutes or until the rhubarb is clear. Test for a set by placing a saucer and a teaspoon in the freezer for a few minutes. Take a spoonful of jam and place on the saucer and leave in the fridge for a few minutes. If the jam wrinkles when you skim the surface, it has reached setting point. Keep boiling until setting point is reached.
4. Sterilise your jars by placing in a hot oven for a few minutes. Ladle jam into warm jars and cover. Leave to set overnight.

Fat Tony

....

Origin
Bristolian.

Recipe supplied by
Julian Mallett of the Windmill pub in
Windmill Hill.

Ingredients
50 ml quality gin
25 ml freshly squeezed orange juice
¼ lime

This recipe was invented for a cocktail
competition held at the Blue Rooms, Bath, four
years ago. I was looking for a name for this
gangster-style gin and juice cocktail. My nephew
Joe, being a massive Simpsons fan, came up with
the name 'Fat Tony' – the godfather of
Springfield.

Method
1. Add gin and juice to cocktail shaker.
2. Squeeze lime and drop into the shaker too.
3. Add lots of ice and shake until the outside of
   the shaker is frosted.
4. Strain into a chilled martini glass and garnish
   with a twist of lime.

TOP TIP
The better the quality of the gin, the better the drink.

cider

Origin
Somerset.

Recipe supplied by
Richard Jones from
Balmain Street and
Sean Busby from
Upper Street who have
lived in Totterdown
since about 1999.

Ingredients
Cider apples

We made our first batch of cider in 2007 using cider apples collected in
Gloucestershire and Somerset. It's a long process, but hugely enjoyable and
the results have been excellent. Wild yeast occurs naturally on the skins of
cider apples, so there is no need to add yeast. You will need a scratter, a
cider press, some brewing buckets and air locks. Cider is traditionally made
from October onwards and the first brews are ready in January.

Method
1. Collect apples, wash and discard any that are obviously rotten.
2. Reduce apples to a pulp using a mechanical or electric fruit mill known as
   a scratter. We use a Fruit Shark electric scratter.
3. Place pulp in a muslin bag in the press. Press the apples and collect juice
   in brewing bucket. Fill brewing bucket to within an inch or so of the lid.
4. Take hydrometer reading. Put the lid on the bucket, insert airlock and
   leave to ferment. Inspect regularly for signs of fermentation.
5. When the hydrometer reading is down to 1000, all the sugar should
   have turned to alcohol and the cider is ready to drink. However, cider
   should undergo a secondary malolactic fermentation in the spring when
   the sharp malic acid is converted to the softer tasting lactic acid, so it's
   worth being patient.

TOP TIP
Allow plenty of time to thoroughly clean all equipment after pressing and to get rid of the pumice
(the solid apple 'cake' left in the press after the juice has been extracted). The pumice attracts fruit
flies so it's best to take it to the dump and put with the green waste immediately after pressing. Or it
can be used as cattle or pig feed, if you have any cattle or pigs.